THE
BLACK
MUSEUM

THE
BLACK
MUSEUM

New Scotland Yard

Bill Waddell

LITTLE, BROWN AND COMPANY

A *Little, Brown* Book

First published in Great Britain in 1993
by Little, Brown and Company

Copyright © 1993 by William Waddell

The moral right of the author has been asserted.

A CIP catalogue record for this book
is available from the British Library.

ISBN 0 316 90332 9

Typeset by M Rules
Printed and bound in Great Britain by
BPCC Hazell Books Ltd
Member of BPCC Ltd

Little, Brown and Company (UK) Limited
165 Great Dover Street
London SE1 4YA

CONTENTS

INTRODUCTION

The Crime Museum at Scotland Yard has been the focus of much attention from the media and writers of both books and newspapers. There is a constant demand for visits by the general public, who as a rule cannot be admitted due to the problems of security and the sheer impossibility of admitting the large numbers who apply. During my tenure of office as Curator I endeavoured to give access to as wide a variety of visitors as possible, but the means do not exist to accommodate all those who express a wish to come due to staff limitations and the physical size of the facility. Each visit takes the form of a lecture, where visitors are given a talk relating to their particular professional discipline. As the primary function of the museum is to teach, the priority for visits must go to police officers, magistrates, criminologists, pathologists, and all those who have the direct task of solving and resolving matters relating to crime.

It is for those people who have expressed a wish to visit the museum and have been refused, that I have written this book in an attempt to describe to the reader a cross-section of some of the exhibits and to provide a valuable reference for the crime historian. Having been involved in the design, display arrangements and the everyday general running of what is one of the most remarkable records of the history of man's selfish inhumanity to his fellow man, I can say that the museum provides an interesting insight into the many types of crime dealt with by Metropolitan police officers, and for that matter by police officers all over the world.

Although the museum will no doubt be changed as the years progress, as it has been in the past, there is one constant that can be found in both the first museum opened in 1874 and the present one opened in 1981. The items on display are the actual relics found at the scenes of the crimes, or in the possession of the criminals involved in the cases, and in most instances are the actual clues which were the focal points for solving those crimes.

The collection has been constantly updated over the years, a tradition which continues today, and in this book you can involve yourself in a visit to one of the most famous and least seen museums in the world – the Black Museum of New Scotland Yard.

How Did Scotland Yard Get Its Name?

Scotland Yard. The name provokes interest; the origins of that name provoke argument.

Old manuscripts tell us that Scotland Yard was 77 ft long, 33 ft wide and was a piece of land that could be rented. Today it can be found lying in the area bounded by Whitehall, Northumberland Avenue and Whitehall Place. It is claimed the Scottish kings stayed here when they came to London to pay homage at the English Court. There are numerous quotes in records to support the fact that a piece of land in the vicinity was used for such a purpose, there is little evidence to confirm that the claim is true. Another and more likely origin of the name can be found in a record which tells us that the church of St Mary Rouncival once stood in the area and that the Prior claimed possession of a nearby farm owned by a man called Adam Scott. Some 200 years later, a tenant of the same piece of land, Cicilie Kelly, bequeathed to her daughter all those lands, meadows and gardens which were known as Scottes Ground. Does the name of the Metropolitan Police headquarters stem from the fact that it was land once owned by Scott – Scott's land; or perhaps the name comes from the old English word for a rent – a *scotte* – bearing in mind that this plot, as stated above, was one that could be rented.

Certainly when Cardinal Wolsey was given this piece of land in 1519, and subsequently built the Palace of Whitehall on it, the area known as Scotland Yard lay within the northern boundary and included the guard room and a number of administration buildings. Many years later these buildings became derelict and when inherited by Charles II after the Commonwealth the area was described as being 'ill built, and nothing but a heap of houses erected at divers times, and of different models'. By 1662 the houses had been renovated and were being used as offices and now we hear of its first connection with law and order. A body called the Commissioners of Scotland Yard, tasked with the job of finding solutions to the lawlessness that prevailed in Westminster, established an office there. When the palace burnt down in 1698 maps showed that there were three yards all with the name Scotland attached to them: Middle Scotland Yard which became Whitehall Place; Little Scotland Yard which was later built on; and Scotland Yard which became what it is today – the street called Great Scotland Yard.

When the Commissioners Rowan and Mayne purchased 4, Whitehall Place as their Central Office in 1829, the rear of the building backed on to Great Scotland Yard and it was from the rear entrance that police officers entered and left the building. They began to refer to their headquarters as just Scotland Yard and to their back entrance as the Back Hall. Today the main entrance to Scotland Yard is traditionally called the Back Hall and the building is simply referred to as Scotland Yard even though its full title is New Scotland Yard.

1

THE BLACK MUSEUM

W hen the Black Museum opened in 1874, it was housed in a tiny second-floor room, in a seedy building that stood in Great Scotland Yard, the thoroughfare that ran between Whitehall and the Embankment.

It was the brainchild of Inspector Neame, the officer in charge of the Prisoners' Property Store, where the belongings of prisoners were kept until they were released from gaol. Prior to an Act of 1869, items used in crime were kept by police until their owners reclaimed them, but the new Act gave authority for police to destroy those objects that had been used, or were likely to be employed again, for criminal activities; it also gave them power to retain other material that could be displayed for instructional purposes. Neame started by gathering together a collection of exhibits that had been found in the possession of burglars and thieves, with a view to mounting a display for instructing police officers about the methods used by these types of offender. Within a year these items were being exhibited in a museum that had been established in a tiny room on the second floor of the store, but instead of displaying just the tools of burglary, it soon became the repository of devices relating to every type of crime committed within the Metropolitan Police area. Today's museum still has many of the original wedges, jemmies and lock picks that were shown by Neame, but the collection has been added to over the years so that today there are artifacts from some 850 different crimes on display, with many more kept in store.

The latest museum is housed on the first floor of New Scotland Yard's tower block, where it was opened on 12 October 1981 by the Commissioner Sir David McNee. Effectively it is a lecture theatre, where the Curator gives talks on the specialised investigative techniques and professional skills used by those involved in the resolution of crime, highlighting each talk with actual case studies. The subject of the lecture is related to the particular discipline of each of the visiting groups, so that police officers for instance can be shown the latest criminal methods, the current status and patterns of crime, or the state of the art in the world of weaponry. Doctors would be more interested in seeing the pathological aspects of the various cases, while the legalities would be highlighted to visiting barristers and magistrates, and so on.

The Old Museum

Visitors to the museum are met by a Reception Officer in the Back Hall, the traditional name for the main entrance to Scotland Yard, and taken by lift to the first floor. A walk along a brightly lit corridor, through a set of double doors, and you find yourself in a dimly lit room that is a reconstruction of the museum as it looked shortly after it had been opened in 1874, the design for which was taken from an old print found in the *Illustrated London News*. As your eyes become accustomed to the gloom, you will see staring down at you from a high shelf that runs around the walls, the disembodied heads of people who have been hanged, chiefly for the crime of murder. These plaster casts, some black with age, were taken directly from the faces of the deceased shortly after their execution, and give us the only accurate three-dimensional likeness of the facial features of many notorious murderers. Here you can see John Thurtell who, in a conspiracy with others, murdered William Weare in 1823 after cheating him out of a large sum of money; James Greenacre who, in 1837, was executed for the murder of Hannah Brown, having dismembered her body and deposited it bit by bit around various locations in London; Franz Muller, the first train murderer who in 1864 killed Thomas Briggs on a train between Hackney Wick and Bow. They represent a unique collection of men and women who paid the ultimate penalty for their crimes.

When a recruit joins the Metropolitan Police he is given a Warrant Number. These numbers have been consecutive since the force began and are now up in the two hundred thousands.

Constable William Atkinson had the number 1. He was dismissed from the force for drunkenness on the first day the police walked out on the streets of London, on 29 September 1829.

Around you in illuminated cabinets are such items as a small sampler cushion, embroidered with the hair of a female recidivist called Annie Parker, who served over four hundred separate sentences for drunkenness, and who spent her spare time in prison doing embroidery work using her own hair instead of cotton. There is a postcard sent by John Lee, the man they could not hang because the trapdoor on the scaffold jammed, and who, after it failed for the third time, had his sentence commuted to life imprisonment. After twenty-two years he was released and went to America, where he died in 1933. Over the fireplace in one corner of the room you can see the Ripper wall, with photographs of the victims and a poster showing the letter that was allegedly received at the time of the murders, and signed with the name Jack the Ripper.

Here also can be seen a magnificent plate camera, made from mahogany with black bellows and brass fittings, the first camera used by police to take pictures at the scenes of crime. There is a clock which was part of an explosive device used by the Fenians. There are the instruments used to take detailed measurements of criminals' facial features, in the days when anthropometry and Bertillonage were in vogue. This was an early attempt to find a method to make identification easier, by comparing the facial features of one individual with another. Your attention will move from these to the other side of the room, where hanging on the wall there is a strange folding ladder. This was used by Charlie Peace, who would climb to the roof of a house, drop the ladder down to a first-floor window, and having secured it to a chimney stack, shin down, drill a hole through the window frame with a wood auger or gimlet, slip the catch and gain entry. Having removed what he wanted, he would climb back on to the roof, fold the ladder, replace it in its attaché case, and leave the scene. The ladder, made of lengths of wood hinged with coach bolts, can be collapsed into a space measuring 9 inches by 16 inches by 3 inches, and even today, over a hundred years later, it represents an ingenious mind.

By now your eyes, well accustomed to the gloom, will focus on a table. This extends around two sides of the room, and on it you can see a bizarre collection of knives, guns and clubs. Each of the two hundred weapons on display have been used in an individual case, to kill or seriously injure someone. The sheer enormity of violent crime starts to come through to you, but before you have time to contemplate, the Curator will take you away from the world of the past and on into the world of the present to that part of the museum that deals with modern crime.

The Modern Museum

Here the cabinets are filled with displays highlighting the crimes of this century. The gun used by Haigh to dispatch his victims, before he disposed of them in a forty-gallon oil drum which served as the acid bath. Items found at 10, Rillington Place, and used in evidence against Christie. A cooking pot used by Dennis Nilsen. But it is not only exhibits relating to individual crimes that can be seen. There are specimens from all the different categories of crime that have been investigated in the course of a day's police work: rape, arson, kidnapping, counterfeiting, espionage, fraud, burglary, bank robbery; the world of drugs. The latter category is today considered to be the focal point of many offences. Crimes are committed under the influence of drugs, or to obtain the money to purchase drugs. This is the depraved sad world of the addicts. Here are the bloodstained syringes they use to inject themselves with heroin; freebasing pipes, used for smoking pure cocaine base, where, to remove the impurities, the drug is heated in a flammable solvent, creating with it the inherent risk of an explosion. This is the world of the 'uppers', 'downers', 'pot', 'smack', 'crack', 'goofballs', 'nose candy', 'sleighrides', 'happy dust', 'kif', the descriptive language of the junkie. The exhibits depict the ingenuity of the pushers and suppliers, for instance, a simple beer can which, when the base is unscrewed, reveals a container which had enough pure cocaine to sell on the streets for many thousands of pounds, and which was discovered because the detective was suspicious of a man carrying a 'fourpack' of different brands of beer. The policeman became curious about the man's difficulty in replacing the cans in their plastic tie once they had been removed, investigated further and succeeded in removing another illegal seller of drugs from the streets.

There is one particular exhibit that always intrigues the visitor. It is a tiny pellet mounted on a pin, inside a glass phial. It measures only 1.53 mm in diameter, the size of a full stop. This tiny object has two holes in it, and it contained the poison ricin that killed Georgi Markov, as he stood on the south side of Waterloo Bridge waiting for a bus.

You are now drawn from one cabinet to another. The Great Train Robbery. The attempted kidnapping of Princess Anne. The Spaghetti House Siege. The Shepherd's Bush Massacre, where three police officers were killed on the same day in 1966. All are cases that caused a great deal of public concern, and achieved notoriety in the minds of the press and the public. To the Yard, these cases represent a great deal of hard detective work.

In 1810 there were 222 offences on the statute for which hanging was the punishment if found guilty. These offences included:

► shoplifting goods worth more than five shillings

► robbing a rabbit warren

► impersonating a Chelsea Pensioner.

But it is the last part of the visit that leaves a lasting impression. You return to the old part of the museum and are given the opportunity of handling the weapons that are used in everyday crime: the variety of guns, knives, and blunt instruments which are dealt with in the course of the routine daily work of the Metropolitan Police. There is a gun disguised as an umbrella, a flexible telescopic cosh, a knife concealed in the buckle of a belt, a pen which releases a seven-inch spike. It is hearing the case histories of each of these items, and seeing how they are used which will leave you with unforgettable memories. For when you leave the museum and return to the world of normality, your mind filled with all those crimes that you have long since forgotten, and when time has dimmed your memory of the visit to the

Yard, you will remember at least one item that you saw on that day when you visited one of the world's most remarkable museums.

The Loving Cup

The Loving Cup was made from the vault of a woman's skull. When it was bought in 1901 by an antique dealer for just £2, it was in a pretty decrepit state, covered in grime, and with one of the handles broken off. He had it repaired and cleaned, and it was presented as a gift to the museum in 1902. The skull has been mounted in silver and from the hallmark it can be determined that it was made in London in 1807.

The cup had apparently been in the possession of a doctor in Berwick-on-Tweed, who had given it to the lady who sold it to the antique dealer. It is accompanied by a number of letters written by this lady, relating the cup's history. She tells the story of a woman of high Irish birth who, when jilted by her lover, went to Edinburgh where she opened a brothel. According to the story, into the brothel some nineteen years later came a student from the university, whom the woman recognised as the son of the man who had jilted her. Memories of her previous humiliation made her decide to kill him, and while making love to him, she plunged a knife into his back.

She was arrested, tried for murder and sentenced to death. One of her last wishes was that her body should be donated to medical science, and after her execution the vault of her skull was removed and mounted in silver in the form of a loving cup.

Although the letters give a very dramatic and plausible story, the facts do not support the evidence. Graphological analysis of the handwriting in the letters shows that the writer had a vivid imagination and there is a strong thread of fantasy running through her story.

One of the problems with the analysis of handwriting is that although it can identify character traits, it cannot be considered an exacting science. It is accurate in only about 70 per cent of the cases where it is used, it often being difficult to determine whether the writer is male or female.

Nevertheless curiosity about the cup's origins prompted me to make inquiries. A check of the records of hangings in Edinburgh showed no trace of a woman being executed for such a crime and with such a history, around the period when the cup was made.

Some marks found on the front of the skull were said to have been made with a trepanning saw (the type of saw once used by surgeons and pathologists to remove the vault or top of the skull). Examination showed that the marks were not caused by a saw but are compression marks similar to those made by a blow from a heavy blunt instrument. This suggested that the woman had died as the result of being hit on the head, death being more likely to have resulted from a sub-dural haemorrhage.

A sample taken by drilling into the bone was analysed, and this did identify traces of blood that had permeated into the layer beneath the surface of the vault, determining that the woman was more likely to have suffered death from a blow on the head rather than dying from judicial hanging. So the story related by the lady in her letters about judicial hanging would seem to be purely apocryphal.

Previous curators of the museum had always thought that the inside of the vault was covered in blood, and a dark brown stain can be seen on the inside surface of the cup, which would suggest this possibility. However, a laboratory test showed that the stain was not blood but in fact the sediment from red wine. This is altogether more appropriate, considering that loving cups were made for drinking out of. Although the idea of drinking from a skull may seem somewhat macabre and ghoulish, these cups were popular in Ireland and Scotland where they were used by cults as part of their strange rituals.

The most likely explanation as to the origins of the cup is that it was probably devised by medical students, who used it in their fraternity rituals.

2

THE DEVELOPMENT OF IDENTIFICATION

As you enter the museum, the first things that attract your attention are the rows of disembodied heads, displayed on high shelves running round the walls — the death masks (and in some cases, the life masks) of people who were hanged at various prisons during the nineteenth century. The original collection was given to the museum in 1878, donated by Mr Howard Vincent, who had been appointed Director of the newly formed Criminal Investigation Department. The collection was added to when Newgate Prison was closed in 1904. After an auction of the prison contents, a number of the plaster heads remained unsold, so the auctioneers donated them to the museum, bringing the total number on display to thirty-seven.

James Greenacre

One of the masks in the museum is that of James Greenacre, who murdered Hannah Brown in 1836 by hitting her on the head with a rolling pin, and then sawing the body up and distributing the pieces in various parts of

London. It is an interesting case because it is an early example of forensic pathology techniques being applied to the solving of a crime.

Capital punishment was abolished by an Act passed on 18 December 1969. There were two moratoria before this, both lasting five years.

The last persons to be hanged in the United Kingdom were Peter Anthony Allen and John Robson Walby (also known as Gwynne Owen Evans) for the murder of Alan West at Workington. Allen was hanged at Walton Prison, Liverpool, and Walby at Strangeways Prison, Manchester, on 13 August 1964, at exactly the same time.

A headless and legless torso was found on Wednesday 28 December 1836 on a building site off the Edgware Road, near where Kilburn High Road station is today. A Dr Girdwood examined the remains and found they were those of a woman of about fifty years of age. The head had been severed from the body partially by sawing and partially by tearing. The torso was wrapped in an old blue cotton dress and pieces of sacking, none of which afforded a clue to the identification of the body. After an inquest at the White Lion Inn at Edgware, a verdict of 'Wilful murder against some person or persons unknown' was brought in, and the body was buried in Paddington churchyard. On 2 February 1837, a head was found floating in Ben Jonson's Lock, on the Grand Union Canal, at Stepney. It was examined by a Dr Birtwhistle, who found it was the head of a woman, and that it had considerable facial damage, probably caused by the lock keeper when he was recovering the macabre specimen from the water. There was bruising of the left eye, and a fracture of the orbit, which he deduced had been caused before death; the head had been removed by sawing through the cervical vertebrae and tearing the flesh. The female torso was exhumed from Paddington churchyard and was found to match perfectly with the head.

The legs later came to light in a ditch at Coldharbour Lane, Camberwell. They had been removed from the body in the same way as the head, having been severed four and five inches from the hip joint. They too matched the torso.

It was 20 March before the body was identified. A Mr Gay, curious about the disappearance of his sister, asked for permission to view what remains there were of the deceased woman. He was shown the head, preserved in spirits in a jar, and immediately recognised it as that of his sister, Hannah Brown. She had last been seen around Christmas Day with Mr James Greenacre, to whom she was to be married before the New Year.

Inspector Feltham, in charge of the investigation, wasted no time in getting the magistrate at Marylebone Police Office to grant him a warrant to arrest Greenacre on suspicion of his having murdered Hannah Brown, and set about trying to find him. In the early hours of Monday, 25 March, accompanied by a police constable, Feltham quietly entered a small house at 1, St Albans Place, Kennington. Climbing quietly to the top of the stairs, he burst into the main bedroom where he found Greenacre in bed with Sarah Gale, and informed them that they were under arrest for suspicion of murder.

The trial commenced on 10 April 1837 at the Old Bailey, the case revolving around the evidence given by the doctors. Girdwood gave proof of scientific fact, to show that the body had been decapitated while Hannah Brown was still alive. Birtwhistle proved that the saw marks were made by a saw that had been found in Greenacre's possession. Their evidence was sufficient for the jury to bring in a verdict of guilty. Greenacre was sentenced to death and was hanged in public at Newgate on 2 May 1837 by the public hangman James Calcott, whilst Sarah Gale was deported to Australia.

The mask in the museum was made by J. Miller of 3, Theobalds Road, and is dated 4 May 1837. There is also an example of Greenacre's writing in the museum, in the form of notes that he passed to his counsel during the trial.

Phrenology

Casts of the heads of people who had been hanged were a fairly common sight in the offices of lawyers and barristers. They could also be found in many medical collections where they were used to illustrate ethnic types and medical malformations. Although there are examples of death masks going back for many centuries, the origins of the masks in the museum stem from the ideas of phrenologists, who believed that character traits could be identified by the examination of lumps and bumps on the head. This idea was conceived by a German physician, Franz Josef Gall (1758–1828), who, working with his pupil and protégé Johann Gaspar Spurzheim (1776–1832), developed the concept that there was a relationship between mental abilities and the shape of a person's head. They divided the mind into thirty-seven characteristics such as avarice, possessiveness, self-esteem, conscientiousness, suavity, and identified these characteristics with certain areas of the brain. These could be found by examining the surface of the skull. The notion was publicised to such an extent that it became fashionable to have 'your bumps' read, and the popularity of this pseudo-science led to it being taught for many years in some of the early schools in Scotland.

It was tried in prisons and mental hospitals in Europe and America, where the idea became widely accepted and employed. Until 1906 it could be found in some American prisons, being used for individual identification. In England it was used in mental institutions until 1936, as a means of profiling the character of patients, although the doctrine of phrenology had collapsed many years before. Simply because there are no areas of the brain that can be identified with a particular human trait, and certainly the shape of the skull has no relationship to the identification of character and features of personality.

So the plaster models of these heads, created by the early anatomists, were to be used to train the officers of the newly formed CID. In 1878 there were few basic skills for a new detective to learn. He was more likely to be selected for his talents as a thief taker, or his ability to remember and identify criminals, rather than his proficiency as an investigator.

When appointed, he would be given some brief instruction on the laws relating to crime, and then be taken to the museum where he was instructed by the Curator Inspector Neame on some of the practical devices used by criminals. He would be shown the heads, told how they represented the faces of classic criminal types, and sent out on the streets to find them. This may have been in keeping with the current ideas on the facial identification of an individual criminal, but as practical instruction it was nonsense.

The previous year, prior to his appointment as head of the CID in 1878, Howard Vincent, a young barrister, had travelled around Europe studying new concepts that were being introduced concerning the methods of finding and recognising criminals, and he was keen to introduce these new ideas into the training of his officers.

It was a book written by an Italian doctor that led to the next development in the identification of individuals. Cesare Lombroso (1835–1909), who became known as the father of criminology, introduced the idea that the criminal was a reversion to primitive man, and that he could be recognised by identifying certain facial features. His early researches, while working as an army surgeon, related to the studies of cretinism and pellagra which were common deficiency diseases found in Italy. In the course of his work he examined and measured some three thousand soldiers in an effort to identify their different regional physical characteristics. Other work and studies in psychiatry and anthropology led to the publication of his most famous work, *L'Uomo Delinquente* (*Criminal Man*). But his methodology was at fault. Although based on first-hand observation, his conclusions were more often arrived at by intuition, and in many cases the results could be attributed to pure fancy.

These ideas of the anthropologists – that criminals could be recognised by physical means – was to lead to the climbing of another rung on the ladder of identification development. There was no way of determining whether an individual who had been arrested for some crime or other had in fact committed a similar offence before. If recognised as an habitual criminal by an experienced policeman who had been involved in prosecuting him or her in the past, fair enough:

> The first Metropolitan Police officer to be murdered while acting in the course of his duty was Police Constable 169 Grantham, on 27 June 1830. While dealing with a dispute in Skinners Street, Somers Town, he was knocked to the ground and kicked repeatedly in the head by Michael Duggan. His wife gave birth to twins on the day that her husband died.

but if they operated in an entirely different location and were arrested on suspicion it was impossible to determine whether they had been caught before for some other offence.

Photography had been introduced. and was used for recording 'mug shots'. These were put into large volumes, each bearing a description of the offence. However, if a person was arrested in one location, sentenced, their photograph recorded, and then they were caught at another location and gave a false name and particulars, there was no way that the photograph could be related to that person, unless they had given the right name. The only way they could be identified and linked with their previous convictions, was by finding someone who had dealt with them before and who could recognise and locate their records. The persistent offenders very soon realised that by giving false information about their names and backgrounds, they could ensure a lighter sentence for themselves, at a time when draconian punishment was the norm rather than the exception.

Without evidence of previous convictions the court would have to consider the matter as a first offence, and sentence accordingly. It was a French clerk called Alphonse Bertillon, working for the Prefecture of Police in Paris, who partially resolved the problem when he introduced a system of measuring that could be used to identify the individual criminals.

He took eleven basic calibrations of the head and limbs and entered them on a card. To this he added two photographs – one full face, another in profile. A *portrait parlé* and description of any special physical features such as warts, scars or birthmarks were included. Bertillon now had an individual record which was filed, and could be used when an arrest was made.

He was given a three-month trial period in which to make his idea work, and fortunately within that time he managed to identify a man who had given a false name. He proved from his records and measurements that this was the same person who had been convicted previously for another offence, under a different name. This caused some rethinking in the minds of many of his critics, and he was allowed to continue with his work. Using his index he managed to identify more and more people, proving that they had criminal records, but it was a slow and ponderous process. However, there was quicker and more accurate method of identifying the individual in the process of development: fingerprinting.

3

FINGERPRINTS

Since the beginning of time examination of the fingers of the earliest hominids would have revealed the intricate patterns of fingerprints. They can be traced through the development of early human beings: Neanderthal, Rhodesian, Java and Cro-Magnon man, to the highest order of the modern mammal – man (*Homo sapiens*). The anthropoid apes, gorillas, chimpanzees, and gibbons, all have them. Representations of them, dating back thousands of years, have been found in Europe, America and Asia, painted on cave walls, carved into rocks, and cut into wood. Sumerian potters as far back as 3500 BC impressed them into their pottery to identify their work. There is evidence of the Chinese and the Japanese using fingerprints thousands of years ago to identify both criminals and legal documents; and the Egyptians used them to seal the confessions of criminals. Examples have been taken from the withered hands of ancient Egyptian mummies. Close examination of the painting *Dance to the Music of Time* by Nicolas Poussin (1594–1665), in the Wallace Collection reveals that the entire surface is covered with them, probably impressed into the primer when it was wet with the left thumb. Thomas Bewick painstakingly engraved the impression of one of his own fingers into a block of wood.

The first person to examine them in detail was an Italian, Professor Marcello Malpighi in 1670, who looked at them under an early microscope. In 1684, Dr Nehemiah Grew published a paper describing them, with a drawing of the ridges and pores. In 1823 Johann Purkinje showed that these ridges and pores at the ends of everyone's fingers appeared in a number of definable patterns which could be classified as loops, whorls and arches. Then in India, in July 1858, William Herschel, an administrator in the Civil Service, found the only way to guarantee a contract was to persuade the parties concerned to make an impression of their hands on the back of the document. Covering the palmar surface of the contractor's hand with ink, Herschel pressed it down on the document. The impression made was the resurrection of an old technique: Herschel had rediscovered the fingerprint.

When he first had the idea there was very little he could do with it. He experimented taking prints from friends, and treating it all as an interesting hobby. Looking at the different patterns made by each impression, it slowly dawned on him that here was something that could be put to good use. Only when appointed as a magistrate and senior civil servant in 1877 was he able to introduce his idea, as a means of stopping families from continuing to draw the pensions of dead relatives. He also used it as a way of registering documents, and introduced it into local prisons as a means of identifying prisoners, but he failed to apply the system on anything other than a local basis. A year later he returned to England to recover from an illness, but his work did not go unheeded. Others were becoming interested in these tiny ridged patterns to be found on the ends of fingers and toes.

While Herschel was at home, convalescing from his ailment, a man on the other side of the world in Japan, had also become intrigued with these maze-like impressions. Dr Henry Faulds was a dedicated missionary, working as a surgeon in a hospital in Tokyo. He had found marks made by the

THE METROPOLITAN POLICE FINGERPRINT BRANCH

FOUNDER
Sir E R Henry Bt GCVO KCB CSI

HEADS OF BRANCH

C H Stedman	1901–1908
C S Collins	1908–1925
W Bell	1925–1926
H Battley	1926–1938
F Cherrill MBE	1938–1953
J Livings MBE	1953–1959
J Godsell MBE	1959–1966
H R Squires QPM	1966–1968
R A Peat QPM	1968–1975
G T Lambourne QPM	1975–1980
M P O'Neill	1980–1981
F E Warboys OBE BA	1982–1988
N E Newson	1988–

ends of fingers on some pieces of ancient pottery. He had studied them and taken a number of samples from various people, using an ink pad. He wrote to Charles Dickens, describing his work and suggesting ways in which the impressions could be used. Dickens forwarded this letter to his cousin Francis Galton, who was conducting studies into anthropometrics, the recording of individuals by measurement of their bodies. Galton in turn took it to the Anthropological Institute who chose to disregard it.

Ignoring the snub, Faulds continued to write letters to various scientific sources propounding his observations, until one was finally published in a scientific journal. This prompted Herschel and Galton to put pen to paper and describe their experience and scholarship in the field.

Consequently the subject now became a matter of scientific and public discourse.

Faulds was disgusted by Herschel and Galton's claims that they had already carried out research and applied the system, and found it impossible to acknowledge their work in the field. He felt that he was the initiator of this new science, even though most of his work had been carried out after, or in parallel with what had already been developed. Galton and Herschel became firm friends, but Faulds would have nothing to do with them. On the other hand, Herschel never really publicised his work. It was only when he read about Faulds' study, that he began to realise that his ideas were worth developing on a wider scale. By the time he came to this conclusion, others were already associated with the concept.

But Faulds had performed a useful service in the development of fingerprinting. He had brought it to the attention of a wider audience.

It was Galton who availed himself of the golden opportunity to publicise the art of dactylography. A histologist and geneticist, who studied human behaviour in all its various aspects, he had travelled widely, written books and published hundreds of papers on various subjects.

In February 1888, he was invited to present a paper to the Royal Institution on the Bertillon system, the physical measurement method for recognising criminals, adopted in Paris by the French Police. He decided he would use the opportunity to bring the art of fingerprinting to the minds of the scientific community. He contacted Herschel and, after some discussion, wrote a paper based on Herschel's experiences with the system. In his talk he explained a way of identifying each print, by describing the three most common patterns found on the surface of fingers: the arch, the loop, and the whorl. To add realism to his presentation, he gave a practical public demonstration of how the patterns could be taken from the hand and how they could be compared.

Galton was fully aware of how valuable this work could be

if perfected, as a means of identifying a specific person. He spent the next six years working on his method publicising ways in which his ideas could be applied. In 1892 he published the first definitive book on the subject, called *Fingerprints*.

While Galton was trying to perfect his system of fingerprinting, Juan Vucetich was working with the Police Department in La Plata, in Argentina. He too was using the Bertillon system of individual identification and realising, like so many others, just how slow and laborious it was to apply. He had read about Galton's work and adapting it as a pattern, devised his own system of classification where he utilised all ten fingers. Getting authority not only to take the fingerprints of prisoners in custody, but to visit and take impressions of prints found at the scenes of crime, he was soon able to use his method to solve a murder. In 1892 he gave evidence of a hand mark found at the scene of the violent death of two children, in a town near Buenos Aires. He proved conclusively that the killing had been committed by the mother, Francesca Rojas, regardless of her allegations that it had been done by a neighbour. Vucetich had succeeded in solving the first murder where the use of fingerprint evidence decided the case.

Working independently but also in parallel with all the others was Edward Richard Henry. He was serving in the Indian Civil Service, and held a number of different posts, each of which had brought promotion. He had been aware for some years of Herschel's work on finger impressions, and when he became the Inspector General of Police in Bengal, he became absorbed in its potential as a means of identifying criminals.

By 1893, he had perfected a refinement of the anthropological system, using a record card with just six basic body measurements instead of the twelve used by Bertillon. To ensure positive identity and as an extra check, he included on his record card a thumb print, and using this system he established an identification bureau. It was very effective, except that those who were responsible for managing the process found it was quicker to use just the thumb print to identify a person, rather than to plough through the ponderous process of physical measurement.

One of the most unusual uses of fingerprints is to be found in a painting entitled *Dance to the Music of Time* by Nicolas Poussin, which is in the Wallace Collection. There are fingerprint marks across the whole surface of the painting. Examination has shown that they were imprinted into the primer when wet and it is thought that they were made with the thumb of the left hand.

Henry decided that the use of fingerprints would be the way ahead and, helped by others in his Calcutta bureau, he concentrated on developing a system of classifying the prints using all the frontal surfaces of the hand.

Meanwhile in the United Kingdom progress in the use of finger impressions as a means of identifying criminals had been delayed by the report of the Troup Committee. In 1894 the committee had accepted the Bertillon system of anthropological measurement as the primary method to be used when identifying individuals, although in their report they did acknowledge the potential of Galton's system of identification by using fingerprints.

As a result of the findings of this committee, an Anthropometric Registry was established, to be attached to the Habitual Criminals Registry, which was transferred from the Home Office to the control of the Commissioner at Scotland Yard. This was a positive step to ensure that criminal records were kept under one roof, and using both indexes it was ensured that the criminal and his record could be matched whenever necessary, but there was still no system for taking impressions at the scene of a crime.

Although it appeared that everything was going well with

this new method of recording and identifying the criminal, it was not the true position. It was becoming increasingly apparent to those responsible for recording and using the measuring procedure, that it had serious shortcomings. First, it was a long and tedious way of finding an individual, as all the measurements on the card had to be checked. Second, it was subject to human error. If the person taking the measurements was not absolutely precise in what he recorded, the system fell down.

The Belper Committee was formed in 1899 to look into the problem. They found that only 18,000 records had been made in the five years of the Registry's existence, and the incidence of them being used as a means of solving crime was low. By December of the following year, they had concluded that the Bertillon system should be abolished and fingerprinting should be adopted.

When Henry joined the Metropolitan Police in May 1901, as Assistant Commissioner, in charge of the CID, the time was absolutely right for him to introduce his refined procedures of fingerprint identification.

Three officers from the Anthropometric Registry were appointed to organise this new department and index, Detective Inspector Charles Steadman, Detective Sergeant Charles Stockley Collins, and Detective Constable Frederick Hunt. On 1 July 1901 they opened the new Fingerprint Department.

It was to be a year before the police were able to first use fingerprinting as the means of solving a case.

There was nothing complicated about the incident when it occurred, just the theft of three billiard balls from a house in Denmark Hill. The investigating officer Detective Sergeant Haynes, found some fingerprints on a window-sill. Steadman and Collins were called and took impressions of them. When checked with police records, the prints were found to belong to a known burglar named Harry Jackson.

Comparing the thumbprint found at the scene with the prints on the record was simple. However, presenting the case at court and convincing a judge and jury, doubtful and uncertain about such a new technique, was likely to prove to be more difficult. Richard Muir, an experienced Treasury counsel, was retained to present the case. He spent long hours studying the background to the new science and preparing his brief.

When the case was heard on 13 September 1902, counsel acting for Jackson predictably pleaded not guilty, and Muir set about proving what was technically a simple case. Collins gave his testimony describing how fingerprinting worked and showed with the help of photographs the similarities between the ten points found on the print at the scene, and those to be seen on the print in Jackson's criminal record. Surprisingly the defence did not attack the graphically presented evidence, and the newly appointed Commissioner, Sir Edward Henry, was in court to hear the jury bring in a verdict of guilty. Fingerprinting as a way of proving criminal guilt had arrived. It was to be another three years before they could repeat Vucetich's success and solve their first murder, by using this new science.

The first recorded female criminal can be found in the writings of Plutarch. The roads around Sparta were infested with bands of robbers and murderers. One of these was a woman called Phaea, who is recorded as being foul both in life and manners. She was nicknamed 'the sow'.

The introduction of this method of finding the criminal brought with it a period of consolidation, but again it became apparent that there were limitations in the system.

With an increase in the world-wide use of fingerprinting and the development of international communications, it became necessary to be able to send copies of prints across the world, so a telegraphic formula was adopted, to ensure that if an original photographic copy of a print was not available, then an adequate and recognisable written description could be circulated. It was found through usage that the four main patterns, devised by Henry, could be subdivided, giving an increased number of recognisable points.

Detective Chief Inspector Battley, in charge of the department and working with a young Detective Sergeant, Frederick Cherrill, set about solving the problems of devising a more efficient index and better ways of recording prints. They devised a better system of measuring prints, identified several different patterns and found a number of recordable factors within those patterns. This wider range of identifiable points made for a much improved index.

Although the Metropolitan Police had adopted sixteen points of identification as a minimum when proving a print, other forces had adopted different standards. It was not until 1948 that a common standard of sixteen points was accepted in Britain, although internationally the number of points needed to prove a print varied.

Today prints are searched for on a computer system, which is quicker, but with the increase in the number of prints on record, there is an increase in the number of prints that have to be searched. Enormous improvements have been made in the ways a latent print can be developed and the difficulties experienced in taking prints from non-absorbable surfaces such as plastic, have been overcome by metal deposition, better powders, the use of infra-red and ultra-violet light, the employment of chemicals and the use of laser technology. All have brought an improvement in finding prints and developing them.

The value of fingerprinting as a tool in the fight against crime is beyond question, and it is a rare event to hear the evidence of a fingerprint officer questioned in court. As a way of finding the culprit it is still as effective as it was when used to find the thief who had stolen the billiard balls.

Those with criminal records have tried to burn them away with acid. Yet when erased like this they re-appear. Others have tried to hide them by having skin grafted over them but the original pore patterns slowly but surely emerge through the graft back on to the tips of the fingers.

Methods have been perfected whereby a print can be raised from the inside of the surface of a glove. The National Collection at Scotland Yard contains some 4,500,000 prints which are constantly being added to and it is estimated that the chances of two people having the same print have been calculated to be 1 in 12 billion.

4

IDENTIFICATION TECHNIQUES USING DNA

'Deoxyribonucleic Acid' is the beginning of a scientific term that contains over 207,000 characters, making it the world's longest scientific name. Not only would it be impossible for anyone to remember, but it would be difficult to pronounce in normal everyday conversation, unless it could be sensibly contracted into an abbreviated form. It is therefore always referred to in scientific shorthand, by just using the initials DNA.

The development of an exciting new technique has enable scientists to identify positively the differences between one individual and another, and although it has been given the title 'Genetic Fingerprinting', it would be more accurate to refer to it as 'Genetic Profiling'.

Establishing a person's identity using their DNA patterns is vastly different to the identification techniques using finger impressions. It all resulted from a discovery made in 1665 by an English scientist, Robert Hooke, who found that solid matter was composed of separate cells, which were bonded together to form the whole. Subsequent research showed that these were the building bricks from which not only humans, but all forms of animal and plant life were constructed. The human body contains billions of these minute living units, each of which can feed, breathe, perform specialised functions, and communicate with other cells.

The cell is often described as being composed of protoplasm, which is a general name given to the substance that is fundamental to life. Each cell has two main parts, a viscous translucent substance called cytoplasm, which surrounds a nucleus enclosed in a film of nucleic acid.

It was in 1911, when Levene discovered that there were two types of nucleic acid: ribonucleic acid (RNA) – Ribose and deoxyribonucleic acid (DNA) – Deoxyribose. DNA is a polymer molecule and is in the form of a double-stranded helix containing thousands of sub-units, and it is from this DNA that chromosomes are made.

Chromosomes are rod-like structures found in pairs within a cell, and it is these which control all the genetic information necessary to form both our own physical being and the forms of all plants and animals.

The cells from which the body is made are constantly dividing and reconstituting themselves, replacing dead or lost tissue. When a cell divides it goes through four phases. First, the Prophase when all the chromosomes lump together in the centre of the nucleus, followed by, second, the Anaphase when the groups of chromosomes moving around within the cell begin to polarise. Third, comes the Metaphase when the chromosomes form into two distinct groups, making the nucleus of two new cells. The fourth and last stage is when the two cells separate completely. This is termed the Interphase.

After the cells have divided, the nucleus will contain a total of 46 chromosomes, 23 of which will come from the male sperm, and 23 from the female ova. In these chromosomes are found the genetic material which determines the physical make-up of an individual, i.e. sex; colour of hair and eyes; shape of nose and face, physical build; 50 per cent of the human being is created from the male characteristics, and 50 per cent from the female.

The DNA helix stores the details about an individual in the form of bits of information which are in sequence, very much as we record any information when writing or printing. It is the analysis of this sequential code that forms the basis of the DNA identification technique.

This was first determined by Watson and Crick who in the 1950s found that the DNA helix was made up of two interlocking spirals which were joined by pairs of bases that formed, as it were, the rungs of a ladder. To picture this, imagine a ladder that has been twisted along its length, and that each rung is in two pieces, each made of different nucleotides or bases.

The four bases in the DNA are:

A = Adenine
T = Thymine
C = Cytosine
G = Guanine

Unlike a ladder where the rungs are solid, in our imaginary ladder where the rungs are made from two different materials, the rungs will not join unless the bases are compatible. A will join with T, and C will join with G, and vice versa, but A and T will not join with either G or C.

What the scientist is searching for is a restriction site, which is a palindromic sequence which occurs at random along the length of the helix. It is the relative position of these sequences that gives the pattern of bands which distinguishes one individual's DNA from another's. These clusters are found in blocks of six, and you get the same order of the four bases in reverse, on the opposite sides of the helix.

For example, a group of twelve compatible bonds would appear as:

```
            A— —T
            C— —G
            T— —A
            _____

            A— —T
            C— —G
            A— —T
            T— —A
            G— —C
            T— —A
            _____

            G— —C
            A— —T
            C— —G
```

The six pairings between the two lines are a palindromic sequence. There are approximately three billion of these bonds in the complete genetic code of a human being, and it is estimated that less than half are required. The purpose of the remainder is not yet fully understood, but biochemists are working on a fuller analysis of the content. The sequence of these millions of bits found within the DNA helix provides us with a meaningless permutation, but it is this genetic blueprint and the identification of parts of it, which have given us a positive means of identifying the criminal and which will in time become one of the most valuable methods of detection to be used by future generations of detectives.

How Does It Work?

The DNA can be abstracted from cellular material and fluids found in the body. It is found in white blood cells, in mucus, in hair follicles, in bone marrow, spermatozoa, urine and faeces.

First, the DNA is chemically extracted from the sample. As we know it is composed of the four building blocks: Adenine,

Thymine, Guanine, and Cytosine. Then it is cut up with molecular scissors in the form of an enzyme. The body's natural defence system embodies certain bacteria which contain these enzymes which are known as restriction endonucleases. They recognise the palindromic sequences in the DNA, and when they do, it causes the DNA chain to break where they occur.

A technique called gel electrophoresis is now used to separate the different-sized pieces from each other. The fragments of the cut DNA are placed in an agrigose gel, and a current is applied across it. This causes the bits of DNA to move through the gel; using a process called Southern Blotting, they are then transferred to a nylon membrane.

It is at this point that the magic of this biochemical process takes place. The membrane is subjected to radioactive probes which cause the pieces of DNA to shuffle around and form into a pattern that is similar to the bar codes found on groceries. Like the bar code which contains information relating to the product and its price and which can be translated by the computer, so the DNA profile can give information about an individual.

The possibilities of DNA had been recognised for a long time before Alec Jeffries, Professor of Genetics researching at Leicester University, found the key that released the secrets of this remarkable forensic technique. The breakthrough came in September 1984, when he discovered a group of probes that would identify a greater number of points on the DNA strands. These multi-locus probes, as they are called, are pieces of DNA material which target and combine with the specific DNA sequences found in the sample. The radioactivity in the probe marks them, and when the membrane is placed next to an X-ray film and developed and printed, the result is the classic DNA ladder profile. These multi-locus proves revolutionised the forensic scientists' ability to recognise one individual from another, which up to that point in time had been the prerogative of fingerprinting.

The first case solved by means of DNA profiling was that

of Robert Melias, who was convicted of rape in November 1987 at Bristol Crown Court. The first murder in this country to be solved using the DNA method to identify the direct connection between the killer and the victim was that of Lorraine Benson in 1988 by John Dunne. The Metropolitan Police first introduced testing in 1989, and now has a fully computerised searchable DNA Database at their Forensic Laboratory.

The system that was originally used for identification in paternity suits is providing an invaluable weapon in the solving of crime.

5

THE FORMATION OF THE CID

It all really began with an out-of-work soldier. In 1713 Colonel Thomas De Veil, who had fought in campaigns in France and Spain with the Duke of Marlborough, found himself at the age of thirty no longer needed for military service, with only the meagre income of a half-pay captain to support himself and his family. So he decided to set up an office in Great Scotland Yard, to advise fellow officers on how to obtain patronage and employment. With his skills as an entrepreneur, his contacts and his acute commercial sense, the business flourished, and after a while he was able to divert his attentions to a question that had interested him for many years: how best could the rule of law be applied to the degenerate and degraded streets of London?

His solution was to study every aspect of criminality. He looked into the types of crime that were common; how they were committed; the criminals themselves; and in particular how the judiciary dealt with offenders.

He realised, as others had before him, that anarchy was the rule of the day, and this was due both to an outdated method of appointing those responsible for arresting the criminals, and the dishonesty of those charged with sentencing them.

Those nominated to enforce the laws were selected under an archaic writ of 1233, which allowed for random selection of law enforcement officers from residents within each of the multitude of parishes that existed in the city and its surrounds. When elected to unpopular positions by the parish, e.g. constable, those with sufficient money simply paid others to carry out the duties they found so disagreeable.

De Veil came to his own conclusions about these problems, and devised methods as to how they could be resolved. To stress his arguments for reform he spoke out in public, drawing attention to the levels of lawlessness and fear that prevailed on the streets of London, placing emphasis on the dishonest and corrupt way they were dealt with by the magistracy. He demanded measures to rectify this situation.

In 1729 at the age of forty-five, De Veil was rewarded for his efforts and given a chance to prove himself. He was appointed a Justice for the Commission of Peace for Westminster and Middlesex, and wasted no time in setting about the task of applying the law. At a time when mob rule prevailed and justice could be bought and sold, his honest and impartial way of applying the law was unheard of, but his intention was to show, by his own example, that the pursuit and prosecution of offenders by firm and fair means was the way to ensure the safety of the public at large. When in 1739 he moved his centre of operations to number 4, Bow Street, a six-storey house he called his 'public office', he had begun a tradition of law enforcement which was to continue in an unbroken line until the present day.

Although not appointed, De Veil came to be considered as the chief magistrate of the metropolis, and his relentless drive to bring about order within his area of authority earned him considerable respect from those who came before him. It was said that during his term of office he was responsible for the transportation or execution of 1,900 criminals. Harsh this may have been, but these were harsh times and severe sentences prevailed. What was important was that he dramatically reduced the amount of crime within the boundaries of Westminster, making it a safer place to live.

There was another development which De Veil pioneered. Where there were doubts about the veracity of a case, he would inquire personally into the circumstances of the crime. He would attend the scene, investigate the incident and, having examined the facts, come to a conclusion based on deduction. Here then was an investigator in the true sense of the word; here was the forerunner of the detective.

De Veil's death in 1744 left a gap, and it would take three years before another strong upholder of the law would be elected to his post, during which time Westminster once again slid back into the law of the street.

In 1740 a group of men and a woman were brought before De Veil, accused of burglary and murder. One of them, William Meers, was found to be carrying a knife with a broken blade.

Evidence was given that the lock of one of the doors of the house from which the property was alleged to have been taken had been forced. One of the accused, Meers, denied the charge, and not satisfied with the evidence presented to him De Veil ordered the lock to be taken to pieces and examined. Inside was found the tip of the blade that matched the knife. Meers was found guilty and sentenced to death.

In 1747 Henry Fielding, aged forty-one, a novelist and playwright, was appointed a Justice of the Peace for Middlesex. A little over a year later, he found himself as the Chief Magistrate at De Veil's old office in Bow Street. His study of the legal procedures made him realise, as De Veil had, that the corrupt practices of those responsible for the dishonest administration of justice had to be stopped, and respect for the law had to be regained. Within his area of jurisdiction, the work of policing was carried out by two thousand unpaid constables, who were nominated by the old system from within the parish where they lived. They were helped occasionally, but not very often, by beadles or bellmen who had been appointed as a form of law enforcement body by Charles II. They were called 'Charleys' and their main use was to walk the streets shouting the hour. Their income was a small salary paid out of parish funds. A reasonable living could be made by these so-called peace officers if they brought offenders before one of the parochially appointed 'trading justices', who dispensed law from their private offices, away from the prying eyes of those who objected to their chicanery. Miscreants were fined according to their ability to pay, the sum involved being divided between the justice, his clerk, and a small reward for Mr Constable, as he was addressed in the court.

Fielding set about reforming this dishonest system. Using his literary skills, he published papers, pamphlets and addresses, drawing attention to it and outlining his proposals for preventing and dealing with the problems of lawlessness in London. The main thrust of his argument was that those responsible for administering the law should be paid salaries from government funds, but he met with considerable resistance to the idea. His first step was to form a permanent body of trustworthy and conscientious constables who were 'actuated by a truly public spirit against thieves', and he found and appointed six householders of good reputation to carry out the task. With the exception of one, all were people who had held the position of Constable of Westminster, and all were dedicated to the common purpose of finding and arresting those who caused harm and distress by their criminal activities.

The team's first duty was to deal with the gangs of cutthroats who roamed the streets of London terrorising its citizens. It is to their credit that within a few days, seven offenders had been arrested and charged. Many who made their livings by robbing and stealing came to the conclusion that if they wanted to remain at large, they would have a better chance if they left the big city for other parts of the country. Some with more serious charges to answer left the country and went abroad, such was the effect of this group of determined men, backed by the firm and fair justice meted out by Fielding. The seven arrested men were tried, and along with many others took that melancholy journey along the Tyburn Way, the route that stretched from Newgate through what is today called Holborn and Oxford Street, to the place of hanging known as Tyburn. Here, near where Marble Arch stands, they were suspended from a permanent triangular scaffold known as the 'Triple Tree'. A salutary example to all who witnessed it.

This small group of law enforcers attached to the Bow Street office became popularly known as 'Mr Fielding's People', and as their reputation grew so they widened their area of jurisdiction. They did not wear a uniform, which caused a certain amount of apprehension in the minds of would-be offenders who were unable to identify them, and they were not paid a salary for their efforts, hazardous though the work was. Instead, after a successful prosecution, they received a percentage of the reward or 'Blood Money' that had been placed on the heads of those who were wanted. If property was recovered they received a percentage of its value. These men were also available for hire, to carry out detective work in any part of the country. For this they received a fee of one guinea a day, plus expenses, and a similar fee was payable if they were hired for private parties. These seven men, working under the direct control of the Bow Street magistrate, carried out their investigations by using methods of detection and inquiry. The results they achieved were out of all proportion to their numbers, and although without doubt motivated by the size of the rewards, they were the first real detective force.

Their reign did not last long. The reluctance of the authorities to pay the reward monies due to them caused their enthusiasm to waver. Fielding, who had been against this method of payment from the first, endeavoured to get them recompense. He failed, and 'Mr Fielding's People' had to be disbanded.

When Henry Fielding died in Lisbon in 1754, London lost a great reformer, but he had sown the seeds of change. His place was taken shortly after by John Fielding, his half-brother, who himself had been a magistrate for four years and was an avid student of Henry's methods. John was only thirty-three when he became the Principal Metropolitan Justice, and he applied even more vigour than Henry to promote the cause of strong positive justice as a way of maintaining law and order. What was even more remarkable, he was totally blind. It was said that once he heard a voice, he never forgot the name of the man to whom it belonged, as many who tried to fool him realised to their cost when they appeared before him in court.

Among the numerous reforms John Fielding introduced was the idea of rotation offices. These were public offices where fair justice would be dispensed, and which were to be chaired by magistrates, who would be paid for their work on the bench. Six of them were actually recruited to deal with the problems of local crime, but when payment from Treasury funds was refused, their honesty became little different to that of all the other 'basket justices' who had preceded them. Once more dishonesty rather than honesty prevailed.

Fielding started to keep records of all the offenders who came before him, and he also introduced the publication of a bulletin for circulation which contained the descriptions of persons wanted, along with a report of their respective crimes. He reformed the watch, and in 1763 introduced foot and horse patrols in his attempts to make the streets safer. The foot patrols remained, but the experiment with the horse patrols was abandoned, mainly because they were not sufficient in numbers, and Fielding found himself once again opposed by the Treasury, who would not allow money to be made available to pay them.

Among his many important reforms, there was one that was to be of great future significance. He re-established the plainclothes detective force that had been disbanded when his brother was in office, and although there was public doubt about the reappearance of these so called 'thief takers', they soon became respected for the positive way in which they dealt with criminals. They were to earn that respect in a new name – the 'Bow Street Runners'.

It is often believed that the 'Runners' wore scarlet waistcoats, but they did not unless it was by personal choice. The sign of their authority was a small tipstaff or baton surmounted by a crown, which carried within it the warrant of their office. Arrests were made by simply touching the person with the tipstaff, and announcing the reason for the arrest.

John Fielding died in 1780. Forty years of his life had been spent striving to change attitudes towards the employment of a peacekeeping force and the introduction of an honest system of dispensing justice; but as before in the case of his predecessors, his death brought with it a return to the old dishonest practices.

Yet progress had been made. Demands were subsequently made on the government, by the public at large, to increase their efforts to find an answer to the lawlessness that prevailed. The problem was placed firmly in the hands of the politicians. William Pitt, besieged by pressures both at home and abroad, tried to bring about a change. He introduced a Police Bill in 1792, as a means of more effectively administering justice. It was passed, and seven police offices were opened in the metropolis, mainly on the sites of the old rotation offices. Each was staffed by three magistrates, who were paid £400 a year to carry out their duties honestly. Attached to each office were six officers paid out of public funds, appointed to carry out the duties of finding and arresting offenders under the direction of the magistrates. The wind of change was at last blowing favourably in the direction of

permanent improvement in methods of applying law and
bringing order on to the streets.

In 1796 Patrick Coloquhoun, another believer in reform,
wrote a remarkable document entitled, 'A Treatise on the
Police of the Metropolis'. It was a treatise which twenty-nine
years later would serve as the model for the organisation of
the 'New Police'. He formed what amounted to the first
police force in this country, with the innovation of the Marine

The title 'Constable' goes back over 1500 years. It is
derived from the Latin *comes stabuli*, which was the
name for the master of the horse of the Eastern Roman
emperors in Byzantium. The name was used by the
Franks as a military title, and was brought to this country
by the Normans. Constables are mentioned in Magna
Carta, as an office invested in those responsible to the
King for ensuring law and order.

The constable today is descended from the function of
officers who were appointed by the sheriff to keep the
peace. The appointment was for one year, and as it was
unpaid it was not an office that was much sought after,
and was often sold to others by those who were
appointed to the post.

Police Institution in 1798. It was an immediate success. The
basic purpose of this new agency was to prevent thieving
from ships. Working in small, well-armed rowing boats, the
police dramatically cut down thefts and pilfering from ships
moored in the docks. Their headquarters were at Wapping, in
the heart of dockland, and it remains their headquarters
today.

More developments were to follow. Mounted patrols were
reintroduced, this time a larger force with fifty-two men and
two inspectors. They were paid twenty-eight shillings a week,

and were given accommodation and a uniform. They were immediately recognisable, the uniform consisting of a black leather top hat, blue trousers, Wellington riding boots, black leather stock, and a bright red waistcoat which earned them the name of 'Robin Redbreasts'. Each carried a pistol, a truncheon, and a pair of handcuffs. They were appointed to patrol a stretch of the highway, and when carriages or other road users approached them they would announce their presence by calling out 'Bow Street Patrol'.

In addition to the horse patrol, London's streets were policed by the foot patrol, formed by John Fielding. They wore an identifiable coat, but did not have a uniform. The river was policed by uniformed river constables, and the Bow Street Runners carried out the plainclothes detective work. The foundations for a permanent police organisation had been firmly laid down.

Between 1780 and 1829 there were eighty riots in London, many of them serious, and it became obvious even to those who objected in principle to the idea that the time had come for radical legal reform. There was a social need for a properly constituted police service.

On 15 April 1829, Robert Peel, the Home Secretary, in the face of opposition, presented the Metropolitan Police Improvement Bill to the House of Commons. His speech to support it was compelling and on 19 June it became law. On 6 July Charles Rowan and Richard Mayne were sworn in as justices and appointed joint Commissioners. Their objective was to form the 'New Police'. In a little over three months, they had organised the recruitment and training of nearly two thousand men. In the evening of 29 September at 6pm, there emerged from the door of the converted servants' quarters at the back of the new Commissioners Office at 4, Whitehall Place, fifteen uniformed policemen including two sergeants and an inspector. They turned left and marching in single file went under an arch that led into Whitehall. There they split into two groups. One group of six led by a sergeant turned left, and walked down Whitehall in the direction of where in years to come the Houses of Parliament would stand; the rest turned right and marched towards where Trafalgar Square is now located. At a number of given points, the sergeant would order a man to peel off on to his predetermined beat. Their primary object was to prevent crime and ensure the general security of property and safety of the public. It is to their credit that within ten years they had overcome the initial public opposition to their formation, and were respectfully referred to as 'Bobbies' or 'Peelers'.

The tiny street they had originally set out from led to the coal wharves on the river. It housed some eating houses, a public house, a tailor's shop, and a fruit-pie maker's; it had a name that was to become respected all over the world – Great Scotland Yard.

The complexities and subtleties of carrying out the work of policing were not at first appreciated by those who had visualised the formation of a police force, or even by those who had the problems of organising and running it. There were areas of police work that were outside the scope of the uniformed man on the street, the image of a recognisable, sympathetic, and helpful public figure that the Commissioners were keen to promote. On one hand these men dealt with the normal law-abiding members of society who went about their business in a legitimate way, and on the other hand there were those who conducted their lives in a devious, deceitful, and disruptive manner. There were certain groups of people who had extremist and idealistic views on how the world of the future should be formed and organised. Their ideals did not always coalesce with the policies of government. Many of the riots that occurred over the turn of the century were contrived to bring down those in power. Few of these groups had anything but anarchy and self-interest to replace the rules of democracy, but some had the purpose of changing the standards and qualities of the lives of those who lived within that community. Their means of achieving these ends were suspect. The early trade union groups were considered by the authorities of the day to be extremist and a threat to the accepted order of things, and they therefore had to be kept under surveillance. There was, in the absence of any other body, an expectation that the 'New Police' would carry out this clandestine work, in order that the government could be kept informed as to who was likely to undermine their authority. Simply stated, there was a need for police to work undercover. Information on covert activities is not easily obtained when those who make the inquiries are wearing official livery, but there was nothing written into the Police Acts which gave authority for policing to be carried out in anything other than a recognisable uniform.

It was a uniformed police sergeant named Popay, from Camberwell (P Division) attached to Clerkenwell (G Division), who was given the thankless task of observing and reporting on one of these early trade union organisations, which called itself the National Union of Working Classes. This group held discussions on their rights and how they could improve their working conditions. Popay, acting on what he thought was good initiative, decided the best way of infiltrating their meetings was to dress in plain everyday clothes and portray himself as a poor out-of-work artist. As a result he was accepted into the organisation without question. The members found him an enthusiastic and articulate supporter of their cause, but although he purported to be one of them he was in fact gathering information about their purposes, intentions, and details of their association with other secret anarchist groups who had their headquarters in the East End of London.

One of the members of this group of radicals was John Furzey, who was walking past King's Cross police station on his way to one of the union gatherings when he saw Popay working in an office. When Popay turned up at the meeting, Furzey confronted and accused him of being a police informer. Popay insisted that he was not an informer and that he had been in the station for a legitimate reason, but

Furzey was not convinced. Hoping to get Popay to respond and show his hand, he put forward a proposal that the group should hold a demonstration to show everyone they had a right to air their grievances in public, however illegal the authorities were likely to consider their actions. The motion was carried, and they made their plans, part of which were to prepare for confrontation should the 'New Police' intervene and attempt to stop the demonstration.

Popay fed all this information to the Superintendent at King's Cross, and the scene was set for a series of events that were to lead to a ban being placed on officers working in clothes other than their uniforms, and delayed the formation of a detective force for nine years.

The meeting was to be held on a piece of open land called Coldbath Fields, in Clerkenwell, on Monday 13 May 1833. Circulars were distributed which called for the abolition of all the institutions: the monarchy, the House of Commons, the Lords, and anything else that represented authority. They were all to be replaced by the elected representatives of the people.

The Home Office immediately declared it to be an illegal meeting, and made an order stopping it. The Commissioners Rowan and Mayne were called to the Home Office and given verbal instructions to the effect that if the meeting took place they were to disband it and arrest anyone who made an effort to address the crowd. If no one attempted to speak, police were not to get involved; in fact even their presence was not to be revealed.

Contrary to the ban, the meeting took place. Thousands converged on Coldbath Fields. Rowan watched the meeting develop from a nearby house, and Popay, who was working in the crowd, fed information back to the Commissioner while he waited.

When a well-known agitator called Mee started to harangue the crowd, Rowan acting on the information supplied by his undercover officers, ordered in seven hundred uniformed men who had been standing by out of sight. In they went to make arrests and disperse the crowd. The mob turned and attacked them with knives, bricks, and cudgels. The police, initially surprised, found themselves in a vicious running battle, and swinging their 18-inch Lancewood truncheons, fought and defended themselves. In the mêlée, PC Robert Culley was stabbed to death, while many other police officers were seriously injured. Numerous arrests were made, including the man who had seen Popay in the police station, John Furzey.

There followed a number of court cases, many of which were thrown out because of the prejudice felt towards this new uniformed force. An inquest was held in the Calthorpe Arms, a local public house, into the death of Culley. The jury, against the coroner's directions, brought in a verdict of 'justifiable homicide'. The jury were then declared heroes, fêted, and awarded medals to celebrate the event.

Furzey was charged with the attempted murder of a PC Brooke, and Popay in giving evidence revealed that police had been working in the crowd in plain clothes. Although Furzey was found not guilty on a technical point of law, the furore that resulted from the news that police could penetrate organisations without being recognised, feeding back information which could be used against those involved, was followed by the accusation that they had deliberately incited the riot.

The government, to placate those who were the most vociferous and had the least to gain from officers working in plain clothes, ordered an inquiry. The Popay Committee was constituted and quickly came to the conclusion that whilst appreciating the need to employ officers working in plain clothes on rare occasions, '. . . as a practice, it was abhorrent to the feelings of the people, and alien to the spirit of the Constitution'. Sergeant Popay for his part was sacrificed to prejudiced opinion. He was given the sack for 'carrying concealment and deceit into the intercourse of private life'. In police history he was one of the first, but certainly not the last, to find themselves made sacrificial lambs on the altar of bigotry and misplaced belief.

So by 1833, the police were obliged to carry out criminal investigations with local officers in full uniform. There was little wonder they were unable to solve the more serious crimes. That was left to the Bow Street Runners, who were not part of the official police, but still worked under the authority of the chief magistrate at Bow Street.

The decade following the introduction of a police service was politically a stormy one for them. Fired at from all sides by politicians and public alike, there was a greater need for the Commissioners to consolidate their position, rather than attempt to spend time and money on areas of policing that required specialisation, such as a detective force.

There were many setbacks in the early years of their existence, but slowly change was taking place. Instead of being hated, this uniformed company of men, with their leather top hats and swallowtailed coats, began to gain the respect of the population they looked after. They were fair and impartial in the way they dealt with the problems that confronted them, and although subjected to a vitriolic press it is to their credit that within ten years they had brought law and order to the streets of London, and reduced the crime rate dramatically. It was a pattern to be repeated all over the country, when police forces were introduced in towns and counties where corruption prevailed over justice.

As the decade progressed the work of investigating crime fell more and more on the shoulders of the local officers in uniform. Contrary to the ideals expressed by the Popay Committee, where necessary, inquiries were authorised to be conducted by officers in plain clothes, but they were used for observation rather than infiltration.

In some cases it became essential for evidence to be based on deduction, rather than reliance on the evidence of witnesses. Convictions were secured by the comparison of marks found at the scene of a crime with tools found in the possession of the accused. The need for specially trained officers to cope with this type of deductive investigation was becoming increasingly necessary. When in 1839 the only group of authorised plainclothes investigators, the Bow Street Runners, were finally disbanded, it became even more important.

It was publicity in the newspapers and periodicals that had been so against the use of officers working out of uniform, that was to lead to the formation of a detective force. The case was a simple one of shoplifting which took place late in the evening of Wednesday 6 April 1842.

Daniel Good worked as a groom for a Mr Sheil, in the stables of his house, Granard Lodge, Roehampton. He had gone to Mr Collingbourne's the tailors in Wandsworth to get a pair of trousers that had been made for him, but he was seen concealing another pair under his coat as he left the shop. He was challenged by one of the tailor's shop assistants, but denied the accusation, whipped up his horses, and drove off up Wandsworth Hill. Mr Collingbourne found PC Gardner, reported the circumstances to him, and with the policeman and the assistant who had witnessed the event went off to Granard Lodge to recover his property. When they found Good, he again denied any knowledge of the theft. Gardner made an initial search of the coach house which revealed nothing, but when he suggested that he wanted to search the stables, Good became very agitated. It was now late in the evening, and with only the light of a candle, Gardner, the tailor and his assistant, along with Mr Sheil's head gardener and another man, began a search of the darkened stables. As they rummaged, Good's agitation became even more acute. Moving some straw bales Gardner saw in the dim flickering light cast by the candle, the torso of a woman. As he pulled away the bales covering her, he found that she had no arms or legs, and the head had been cut off. These were later found burnt to ashes in the tack-room fireplace. By the time they had recovered from the initial shock of finding the torso, Good had sidled out of the stables and locked the doors from the outside. By the time they managed to force them open,

Daniel Good had disappeared. Gardner immediately sent for his superintendent at Wandsworth, and then questioned a boy who had been found in a room over the stables. The lad told him that Good was his father, and that he usually lived with his mother at South Street in London. When Superintendent Bicknell turned up at the barn at midnight with an inspector, a sergeant, and a police surgeon, he did not react to this horrific murder with any degree of urgency. He ignored the piece of important information, about the house in South Street where Good had in fact gone, and which could have led to his early arrest, and failed to write up his route paper until the following morning. Route papers were brief reports of the known facts of a case that had to be circulated as soon as possible to the superintendents of all surrounding divisions or those most likely to be involved. They could then decide whether to instigate their own inquiries.

When the inquest on the body was opened on 8 April, Bicknell was questioned by the coroner as to why he had not dealt with the case with a greater sense of urgency and purpose. Unable to account for his lethargic approach, he was criticised in court for his lassitude in not circulating the information, which might have led to Good's quick arrest.

The press had a field day. Having heard the evidence in court, and thinking that the police inquiry had not begun, they arrived at the house in South Street where the boy had been living, only to be told that the woman who lived there was not his mother. More sleuthing led them to Molly Good, the boy's real mother, who lived in Bethnal Green. Other inquiries revealed that Daniel Good was a man who had associations with many women. The papers were full of it, giving the impression that they had more information about the case than was known to the police.

They were too late. Mayne had pre-empted the press. When the route papers had arrived on his desk, to say he was furious about the delay is to put it mildly. Only a month before he had circulated a police order informing superintendents of the need for greater diligence relating to the circulation of route papers. When he heard about the Good case late on Thursday, he called in one of his Scotland Yard inspectors with a bent for detection: Nicholas Pierce, along with Sergeant William Gerrett, from 'A' Division. They were given the task of finding Good as quickly as possible, and told not to bring attention to themselves.

The rental of 4, Whitehall Place in 1829, which became the first Scotland Yard, was £560.6s per annum. Today the rental of the present Scotland Yard in the Broadway runs into many millions of pounds.

While the inquest was going on, they had interviewed the boy, seen the remains of the body; and learnt that a woman had been given some of the dead woman's clothes on the morning of the day the body was found. They had been to the house where the owner of those clothes lived, in South Street, London, and found it had been rented by a woman called Jane Jones, who was obviously the victim. By Saturday morning Pierce had tracked down the real Mrs Good in Bethnal Green, and learnt that her husband had stayed with her for two days after he had escaped from the scene, and the last she had seen of him was in a coffee house, where he had left her.

Although the press interviewed Mrs Good, and she told them that she had already been interviewed by two police officers, no one picked up the fact, even after Pierce gave evidence at the renewed inquest to identify the body, that the policemen were working in plain clothes.

Vilification of the police and their actions in the case came to a stop when, twelve days later, an ex-policeman from Wandsworth, Thomas Rose, saw Good working as a builder's labourer in Tonbridge in Kent. He was arrested, and it was found that the folded cloth with which he padded his shoulder when carrying the hod was bloodstained, and although it could not be tested scientifically it certainly carried weight at his trial at the Old Bailey in front of Lord Denman. He was found guilty of murder and hanged at Newgate by William Calcraft, in front of a very large crowd.

The press did not remain quiet for long. While the newspapers were still criticising the inability of the police to catch criminals, a PC Timothy Daly was shot dead in Highbury and two attempts were made to shoot the Queen. The newspapers debated loud and long in their articles and editorials, and the Commissioners – tired of unjustified criticism – decided to take action. It had been realised for a long time that it was an impossible task to try to detect crime without a plainclothes detective force, however unpopular it had been decreed by the restrictions laid down in the Popay inquiry in 1832. After all, the first two of the primary objects defined by Mayne and Rowan when the police were formed in 1829, and learnt subsequently off by heart by generations of future policemen, stated:

> The primary object of an efficient police is the prevention of crime.
>
> Next, that of detection and punishment of offenders, if a crime is committed.

The important word was 'detection'. Nothing had been written or discussed to formulate a policy on how to carry out the work of detection. On 14 June 1842, a memorandum was presented to Home Secretary Sir James Graham by the Commissioners, asking for the formation of a Detective Branch, which they suggested should comprise eight sergeants and two inspectors. Authority was granted four days later. Discussions ensued, and it was agreed that there would be two inspectors and, initially, six sergeants. The sergeants would be paid four shillings (20p) a day, and the inspectors £200 per annum – total cost £984, to be met out of general funds.

The original members of the detective force were:

Inspector Nicholas Pierce	('A' Div.)
Inspector John Haynes	('P' Div.)
Sergeant William Gerrett	('A' Div.)
Sergeant Stephen Thornton	('E' Div.)
Sergeant Shaw	('R' Div.)
Sergeant Braddick	('F' Div.)

Immediately promoted to the rank of sergeant were:

PC Jonathan Whicher	('E' Div.)
PC Goff	('L' Div.)

They were joined shortly afterwards by:

Sergeant Shackell
Sergeant Field

These men were the original detectives in what became known as Central. The only amendment to this arrangement was an authority given by Rowan in 1846, when he permitted two men on each division to be trained as plainclothes officers, presumably as a reserve or replacement in the event of retirement or illness There was to be no change for many years in the numbers employed in this pool of detectives working from the Commissioners' Office. It was kept at two inspectors and eight sergeants until 1864, when authorisation was given for an increase. Another seven detective sergeants were appointed to Central, bringing their number to fifteen. It was to remain at this ridiculously low figure until 1869.

As the years passed it became apparent that there was a need for more manpower to deal with an ever-increasing crime problem. This led Sir Edmund Henderson, on his appointment as Commissioner, to reorganise the number of men permanently employed on detective duties. The two trainees on each division were made permanent and Chief Inspector Frederick Williamson was appointed as the officer in charge.

The instructions the new detectives received in respect of their duties were limited, efficiency being mainly dependent on knowledge accrued by experience and enthusiasm for the work. To increase their awareness the Commissioner gave authority for a collection of burglars' tools collected by Inspector Neame in the Prisoners' Property Store to be shown as a permanent collection for the instruction of police officers, and so the Black Museum came into being.

Gradually the size of the detective force expanded until in 1878 it stood at 123 men; but the events which were finally to bring about the formation of the Criminal Investigation Department were soon to begin.

Money is a focal point in most crimes. Greed for money leads to dishonesty and violence. When that path of dishonesty is trodden by a member of the police force, the wrath of public feeling that follows is crushing. A little of that outrage is felt by every working police officer, irrespective of whether involved or not, and it erodes some of the trust and esteem in which they are held by the public.

Williamson had four chief inspectors working directly under him at Scotland Yard. Three of them together with an inspector were to be arrested and charged with unlawfully conspiring to obstruct, defeat, and pervert the course of justice.

William Kerr was an exponent of the art of creating wealth. His method was to set up an office with an impressive address; have circulars printed and advertisements placed describing how a lot of money could be made by investing in his foolproof gambling system; distribute leaflets in areas away from where his temporary office had been set up, to discourage visitors from inquiring as to the whereabouts of their money; then he would wait for the money to roll in from the

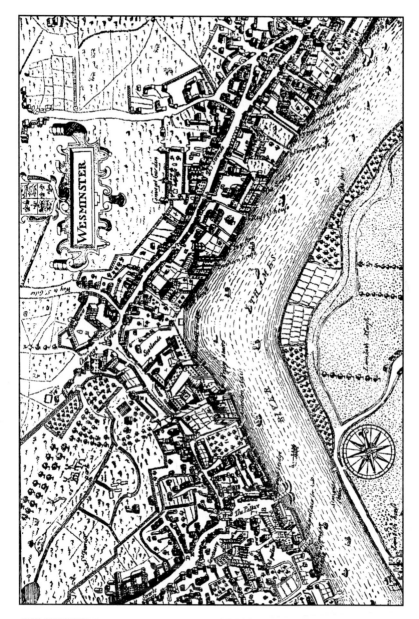

CHAPTER 1

Norden's map in the Survey of London 1593 showing the position
of Scotland Yard.

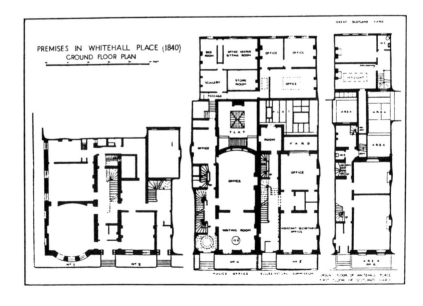

PREMISES IN WHITEHALL PLACE (1840)
GROUND FLOOR PLAN

Opposite Top Left The front of the original Scotland Yard at 4 Whitehall Place before it was demolished in 1929. In this house the first Commissioners Sir Charles Rowan and Sir Richard Mayne, set up their office.

Opposite Top Right Early picture of a policeman in uniform. The top hat was reinforced with cane so that he could stand on it and look over the heads of a crowd.

Opposite Bottom Plan of the original Scotland Yard. The offices that backed on to Great Scotland Yard, were used as the police station.

Above The last of the 'Charlies'; introduced by Charles II, he carried a lamp and a cutlass and walked the streets calling the hour.

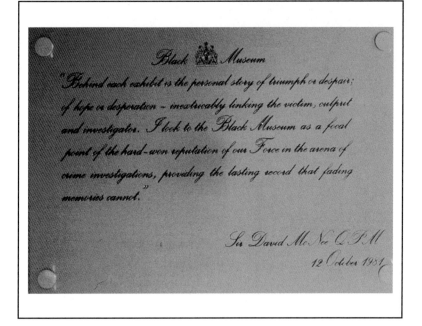

CHAPTER 2

Top Left Hand drawn poster showing the opening times of the museum in 1892.

Top Right Print of the original museum published in 1883. This was used as a model when designing the present museum which was opened in 1981.

Bottom Engraved plate at the entrance to today's museum.

Opposite The new Scotland Yard building on the Thames Embankment opened in 1890, and occupied until 1967. It is now used as government offices.

CHAPTER 3

Top Left James Thurtell hanged for the murder of William Weare 1823.

Top Right Elizabeth Brownrigg hanged for the murder of a servant by whipping.

Centre Franz Muller, the first train murderer, hanged in 1863.

Bottom Left Frederick Deeming, hanged in Australia 1892.

Bottom Right Death mask of Heinrich Himmler, taken after he committed suicide in 1945.

CHAPTER 4

Right Alphonse Bertillon.

Below The Bertillon system of measurements.

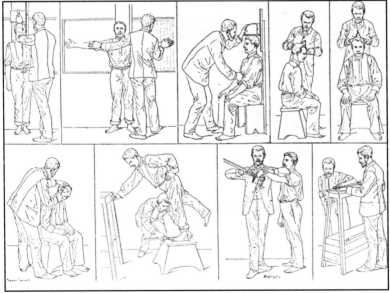

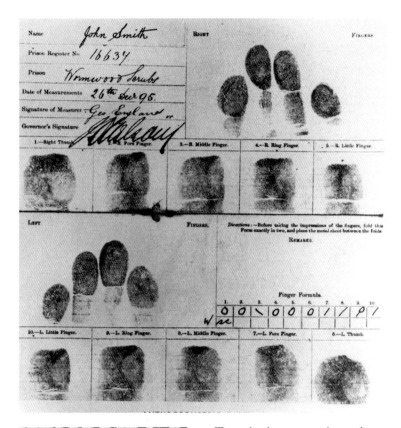

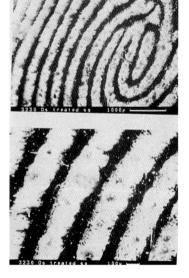

Top Anthropometric card, showing fingerprints being recorded before they were officially introduced as an accepted method of identification in 1901.

Left Enlarged fingerprint showing the pattern or ridges.

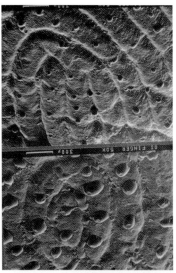

Left Enlargement of print showing the pores which exude the fingerprint deposit.

Below Dusting a silver bowl to identify latent prints.

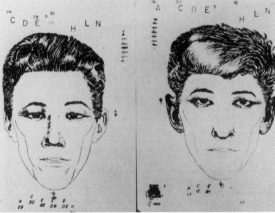

Top Left Checking fingerprints against the records.

Top Right Plaster casts of footprints which identified the murderer Leslie Stone in 1937.

Centre The Identikit picture made and used in the UK to catch the murderer Edwin Bush in 1961. It was made on the first day that the system was introduced.

Left Edwin Bush hanged for murder.

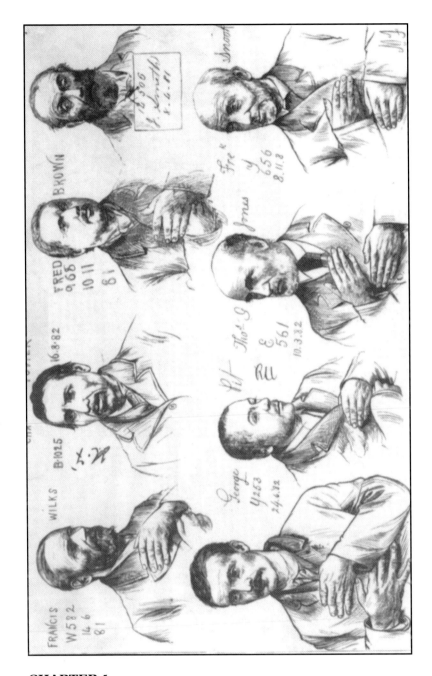

CHAPTER 5

Criminals in various poses for the camera.

Top The convicts' office where criminals who were released on tickets of leave had to report.

Bottom Group of senior detectives taken at Scotland Yard in 1912.

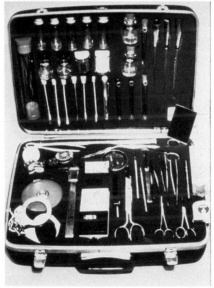

Top The original Big Four of Scotland Yard.
Left to right: A.V. Hawkins, F.P. Wensley, F. Carlin, A. Neil.

Bottom Murder bag used at the scene of a crime in the 1960s.

CHAPTER 7

Left Charles Peace.

Below His unique ladder. Also the false arm and dark glasses that he wore to disguise himself and the small candle lamp he was using when he arrested.

Top The ladder folded to fit into an attaché case.

Middle The museum has a collection of letters written by Charles Peace when he was in prison.

Bottom Jemmies and keys – the tools of his trade. The crucible was used by Peace to melt down items of gold and silver. He never used a 'fence', disposing of his stolen goods himself.

The museum cabinet of Charles Peace, with displays of other 19th century crimes.

avaricious investors. His next course of action was simple. Having got the money he disappeared with it, leaving behind a lot of disappointed punters.

Kerr met up with another fraudster called Harry Benson and together they set up a number of these offices in various parts of the country. Having reaped the profits of gullibility, they would disappear, only to reappear somewhere else. Their dealings soon came to the attention of Scotland Yard, but by then one of Central's select band of detectives, Inspector John Meiklejohn, was in Kerr's pocket, and being paid regularly for supplying information that kept the fraudster one step ahead of his creditors. In turn Chief Inspector Nathaniel Druscovich, who was investigating the movements of Benson, was obliged to borrow money to pay a debt on a bill he had guaranteed for his brother, and Meiklejohn persuaded him to borrow the money from Kerr. He too was now in the pay of the two fraudsmen. It took a few more years for Chief Inspectors Clarke and Palmer to be compromised, and now the two villains were free to carry on with their dishonest schemes, knowing that they had the officers who would be responsible for carrying out any investigations against them in the palms of their hands. All had been drawn into an entanglement of dishonesty and bribery.

Williamson, initially unaware of the web of deceit that surrounded him, had a stack of complaints on his desk demanding action and he put Druscovich in charge of the inquiry. Although the latter managed to prevent the arrest of Kerr and Benson for a number of years, the villains became too greedy and were finally apprehended for a fraud amounting to many thousands of pounds. At the ensuing trial, they were sentenced to imprisonment. Even then the dishonesty of the detectives was not revealed, except that Williamson realised that the delay in bringing the two crooks to justice was a result of inaction by his detective chief inspectors and so he initiated an inquiry into their activities.

The four detectives were duly arrested, charged and put on trial. The hearing at the Old Bailey lasted nineteen days, and for a while held the record of being the longest criminal trial. Meiklejohn, Druskovich and Palmer were found guilty, along with Edward Froggett, a solicitor who had stood trial with them. Clarke was found not guilty and released.

The guilty parties were all sentenced to two years' hard labour. The publicity given to what became known as the De Goncourt Turf Fraud had the effect of raising a government commission for the purpose of reorganising and inquiring into the state of the detective force. The four elected members of the commission held their first meeting on 22 November 1877, while the trial of the detectives was still in progress. They came to the quick conclusion that the head of the new Criminal Investigation Department would be an assistant commissioner but not a policeman. They wanted a man who was 'an astute and experienced lawyer', and found him in a young barrister, Mr Howard Vincent. Astute he was, experienced he was not. Seeing his opportunity for betterment, he immediately went off to Europe to study the latest methods of detection.

In 1877, the most advanced detective organisation was in Paris. There, they had experimented with the latest ideas in criminology, which centred round the anthropologists' premise that if you looked like a criminal, you probably were one. They had also explored various methods of identifying individuals. Vincent avidly absorbed what experience he could, and wrote a lengthy report outlining how he thought the new CID should be organised. He presented it to the committee in January 1878, and applied for the new position, not as an Assistant Commissioner but with a title suggested by himself: Director of Criminal Investigations. He was appointed on 6 March.

The report was redrafted numerous times until when finalised, Mr Vincent was not named as the author. Some of his ideas were to prove to be fatally flawed. One of his suggestions was that the head of the CID should not be responsible to the Commissioner, but should report directly to the Home Secretary. Another proposal was that his force of detectives were to be independent of the police force of which they were in fact part; and what was to cause more problems within the force, they were to receive higher rates of pay than their uniformed colleagues. Vincent had succeeded in building a high wall of élitism within the force, and it would take nearly a hundred years to knock it down.

On Saturday 6 April 1878, the Police Order was issued giving the enhanced rates of pay and the new rank structures. On the following Monday 27 men, from chief superintendent (Williamson) down to 17 second class inspectors, were appointed to Central, to work from Scotland Yard, complete with their own administrative back-up. Some 174 inspectors and sergeants were appointed to work on divisions. They were to be assisted by 80 patrols.

The Criminal Investigation Department had arrived. It had taken forty-nine years from the inception of the Metropolitan Police to form a force that could effectively deal with crime and criminals. It was to prove a success, but it was certainly to have its problems again in the future.

6

CHARLES PEACE

In 1878 the newly formed CID needed a good case to prove their worth in order to dispel much of the scepticism levelled against them concerning their ability to solve crime and to give themselves the opportunity of gaining credence in the eyes of the public. Charles Peace was the answer to their problems.

Peace was born on 14 May 1832 in Sheffield, the son of an animal trainer. Physically he was a very small man, only 5 feet 3 inches tall, but wiry and physically strong. He had what was described as a monkeyish face, and could when necessary contort his features to such a degree that he could render himself unrecognisable – an attribute which he would use to good effect during his career in crime. His father ensured that he had at least a rudimentary education so that he could read and write. Lessons in playing the violin gave him another skill that would serve him well in his future life.

An accident in a steel mill when he was fourteen left Peace with a permanent limp. The outlook was bleak for there was little future for people with such disabilities. However, he overcame his disadvantage by finding work in fairs and public houses, performing with troupes of actors, and playing his violin to entertain. He was advertised as the Miniature

Paganini or the Great Ethiopian Musician and made money by playing at soirées and parties, and giving renderings of famous speeches from Shakespeare.

When not working honestly, Peace turned to crime. In 1851, aged nineteen, he was given his first taste of prison: one month for burglary. When released he continued his thieving activities but succeeded in avoiding arrest for nearly three years, when he was again taken into custody and given four years' penal servitude for his favourite crime: burglary. When once more released it appeared that this long period of imprisonment had taught him a lesson, for he married widow Hannah Ward and settled down to work as a framer and gilder, a trade he had been apprenticed to when young.

To all outward appearances he now led a respectable life. He was quick-witted and intelligent, with a knack for engaging people in conversation; he was a regular attender at church and chapel, even helping as a teacher at the children's Sunday School. However, all this *bonhomie* disguised his real intentions. His readiness to engage in conversation was a ruse to glean information about houses and their occupants, while his violin concerts gave him entry to those houses that he intended to burgle. His violin case was a useful aid, for in it he could carry his house-breaking implements without arousing suspicion.

The good life did not last long. In the same year that he married Hannah, he was apprehended again and given six years' penal servitude for a house-breaking offence at Rusholme. Again, within a year of his subsequent release from prison, he was arrested once more. This time no lenience was shown, and he was given seven years' penal servitude for a burglary at Manchester.

When necessary Peace could give a plausible impression of being a very humble and servile man, and with this Uriah Heep image he managed to convince the Parole Board that he had changed his ways. He was given a ticket of leave, which meant an early release, on condition he reported regularly to a police office.

By 1872, a year before his full sentence had been served, Peace was a relatively free man. When he came out of prison this time, he was forty years of age, and had spent a total of some sixteen years inside. He was determined that it would be a long time before he got caught again, and for the next eight years he led a charmed existence. Although he went back to his old occupation as an entertainer, he was still involved in his thieving activities but managed to avoid capture. He obtained a gun and while practising with it managed to shoot off a finger on his left hand. The gun was to be his guarantee against further arrest, and he was prepared to use it if necessary.

By 1875 he had moved to a cottage in the village of Darnall, where he met a civil engineer named Arthur Dyson. Peace became infatuated with Dyson's wife Kathleen. We can only speculate as to whether she returned his affection, but there is some evidence to show she was flattered by the attentions of this ugly little man. What is clear, is that it was not an association she wanted to continue, and she tried to get rid of Peace by ignoring his persistent advances. Her husband resented Peace's intentions and warned him to stay away, but this did not deter him and he persisted in the pursuit of his paramour. Frustrated by Kathleen's apparent lack of interest he threatened her with the gun and promised to shoot her and her husband. Dyson, fed up with this unwarranted intrusion into his life, took out a summons against Peace to try and get him bound over to be of good behaviour. When called before the magistrates to answer the accusation, he did not appear. For the moment he had gone to ground but was not far away.

On the night of 1 August 1876, PC Nicholas Cock was patrolling in the Whalley Range area of Manchester. While walking along Seymour Street, he saw a man in the garden of a large house. It was Charles Peace. When Cock challenged him, Peace's answer was to pull his gun and fire two shots. The first shot missed, but the second hit the young policeman in the chest and he fell to the ground. Before he could be given help, he was dead.

There were no witnesses to the killing, but it was known that the three Habron brothers, who lived locally, had threatened to kill Cock. As prime suspects, they were arrested for the crime. Two of them, William aged eighteen, and John, twenty-three, were charged with the policeman's murder and stood trial at Manchester Assizes. The proceedings lasted only two days. John was released, but William was sentenced to death. Fortunately he did not hang – his sentence was commuted to life imprisonment because of his age.

The scaffold known as the Tyburn Tree was erected in 1571 near where the junction of Marble Arch and Edgware Road stands today. It was popularly known as the 'Triple Tree' and was a permanent structure, triangular in shape and standing eighteen feet high. It was possible to hang eight people on each of the horizontal beams. The Tree was demolished in 1783 and on that one spot over the some 200 years of its existence, it is believed that over 50,000 people were hanged.

Its position was at one time marked by a small triangular stone in the centre of the road north of the western end of the Arch, but there is now a large plaque set on an island in the centre of the Edgware Road, at the junction. The definite positioning of the Tree has been in contention for many years, there being at least eleven claimed sites.

Peace, devoid of any sense of conscience, sat through the whole trial and watched someone else convicted for the crime that he had committed. Afterwards he commented that 'It greatly interested me. I always had a liking to be present at trials.'

The day after witnessing this travesty of justice, and knowing that the Dysons hoped to get away from him by moving to a new house at Banner Cross in Sheffield, he followed the furniture cart to the new address. When the Dysons arrived at their new home, Peace was calmly sitting in one of their chairs waiting for them: 'You will never escape me. I will always find you.' It was not an idle threat: it was one that was to end in murder.

At 9pm on 9 November 1876, Mrs Dyson came out of the house to go to the outside lavatory. As she walked down the passage that led to the back yard, Peace jumped out of the dark and grabbed her. Her screams drew the attention of her husband, who rushed to find out what was happening. As he ran into the passage, Peace, finding himself cornered, pulled his favourite weapon from his pocket. There was a loud report and Arthur Dyson fell to the ground with a bullet in his head. He died two hours later.

Peace was now a wanted man. Posters offering rewards for his capture were circulated all over the country. Police everywhere were looking for him.

First he made his way to Hull, where he stayed for a short while with his brother. While police were knocking at the front door making inquiries as to his whereabouts, Peace was leaving by the back. He decided to leave the area and take a train to Nottingham. Acting on a tip-off, police boarded the train to search for him. They did not realise that the well-dressed, excited little white-haired old man who ran up and down the train with them while they searched, shouting for Charlie Peace to come out of hiding, was the person they were looking for.

At Nottingham he went to the house of his mistress, Sue Bailey. Again he missed being caught. Police called when he was in bed with her. She kept them talking, while Peace escaped once more, this time through a window at the back.

Peace now thought it would be a good idea to return to Hull, as the authorities had probably given up looking for him thinking that he had left. He was right. He and Sue Bailey, calling themselves Mr and Mrs Thompson, found lodgings with a police sergeant in Aubury Road. This was the perfect cover for his activities, and while living there he carried out a series of burglaries. He realised that things were becoming a little too dangerous, so he decided to travel to London where he bought a house at 5, Evelina Road in Peckham. Here he was joined in a convenient *ménage à trois* by his long-suffering wife Hannah, stepson Willie, and his mistress.

Again Peace became the epitome of respectability. Neighbours enjoyed invitations to the Thompsons, where they were entertained by Peace on his violin, while his mistress accompanied him on the piano. They did not realise that the 'lodger' and her son were in fact Peace's real wife and stepson.

Needless to say, there was an increase in the number of burglaries in and around the Peckham area, many of them being displays of sheer audacity. On his house-breaking expeditions, Peace would carry with him a ladder hidden in what he called his music case. The ladder was an example of Peace's ingenuity. Unlike a normal ladder with rungs, it was made of lengths of wood 2 inches wide and ½ inch thick. These were cut into 15-inch lengths. At one end of each length a groove was cut, and each piece was attached to the other by a coach bolt secured by a locking nut. This enabled the ladder to be folded into a compact square, which would then fit neatly into a small case. Peace would climb on to the roof of the house he intended to enter, unfold the ladder and tie it to the chimney stack with a rope, lower the ladder down over the side of the house to the windows of the top floor. Peace, being an agile man, would climb down by using his toes to balance on the ends of the pieces of wood and use his fingers in the grooves to gain a purchase. He would climb down to a selected window, drill through the frame with a wood auger or gimlet, spring the catch, and gain entry. He would leave by the same way, folding the ladder and replacing it in the case, then walk away from the scene using one of his many disguises. He would wear a false arm with a hook at the end, dark glasses and walk with a limp. Peace also dyed his face with walnut juice and could contort it. There was little chance of anyone recognising the bent shuffling little figure as he left the scene of his exploits.

On 10 October 1878, in the early hours of the morning, PC Edward Robinson was patrolling with PC William Girling, and as they walked along St John's Avenue just off Blackheath, they heard a sound at the back of number two. They climbed up and looked over the garden wall and saw a dim light in one of the downstairs rooms. When it was immediately extinguished, they decided that one of them, Girling, would go round to the front door and knock up the occupiers, while Robinson would remain concealed at the back to see whether anyone came out. Girling met Sergeant Brown, who was also patrolling, and together they went to arouse the tenants. The jangling of the doorbell in the quiet of the night made Peace jump and he quickly climbed out of a window, only to find himself confronted with the figure of PC Robinson. He pulled his gun, and pointing it at the advancing policeman threatened to shoot him unless he kept his distance. As the determined Robinson walked forward, Peace fired once, then twice, then a third time, and yet a fourth time. As Robinson rushed him he fired a fifth shot which struck the brave policeman in the arm.

Robinson grabbed Peace and wrestled him to the ground, shouting for assistance. Girling ran quickly to his aid, and struck the gun from Peace's hand with a sharp blow from his truncheon. Although the policemen did not know it, they had captured the most wanted man in the country.

When he arrived at the police station Peace told them that his name was Ward, and he was charged under that name for the attempted murder of Robinson. He appeared at the Old Bailey, where on 19 November he was given penal servitude for life. Still no one realised who they had caught, until his mistress gave away his identity.

Peace made one last attempt at avoiding the inevitable punishment. It was decided that he should be moved from Pentonville Prison and taken up to Sheffield to stand trial for the murder of Dyson. On the journey north, although he was handcuffed, he managed to relax the attention of his guards and dive out of the carriage window while the train was travelling at over 40 mph. Although the warden managed to grab his legs, he struggled so violently they had to let go, and he fell head first on to the side of the track. The train was stopped and the warden ran back to find a dazed Peace, apparently little worse for the experience.

The preliminary hearings were held at Armley Gaol in Leeds, where Peace constantly complained and whinged and moaned about his treatment and the injustice of it all. At his trial at Leeds Assizes on 4 February 1879 the judge showed little sympathy towards this heartless monkey of a man, who continued to try to invoke the sympathy of the jury with the pathetic picture he presented sitting in the dock wrapped in a blanket moaning about how ill he was.

Peace was sentenced to be hanged by the neck until he was dead. In the end, he did show one last moment of compassion. Before he went to the scaffold he admitted killing PC Cock at Whalley Range. William Habron was released and given £800 for the inconvenience of nearly three years' imprisonment.

On the morning of 25 February 1879, a cold wet day, Peace was escorted to the scaffold. William Marwood, the official hangman, pinioned his hands and feet, placed him on the trapdoor, and put the noose around his neck. At 8am, he pushed the lever and Peace fell to his death. He showed little repentance at the end, but his last words had a grim ring of humour in them.

'The great mistake I have made in my career is that I have used ball cartridges. I ought to have used blanks.'

1

JACK THE RIPPER

When researching into murder, one enters a world of repulsive and macabre happenings, and sooner rather than later one is drawn to read about Jack the Ripper.

This series of crimes committed, some say, as early as 1887, and others as late as 1891, have been the subject of numerous books, which have propounded theories as to why they were committed and by whom, and which have only succeeded in producing a wealth of uncertainty and doubt about the case. The fact is that the trail is cold. Policemen, criminologists, writers, broadcasters, reporters have all made attempts to find the person responsible for these horrendous crimes, yet none have succeeded in producing positive proof as to his identity. In some cases the finding of a new document has led to a spate of interest, usually with as many arguments being presented as to its authenticity, as those which argue its inaccuracies. Numerous suspects have been put forward, some of the claims being supported with convincing evidence, yet each book and article has a different angle which only adds a little more to the myth. Some books are meticulous in their research, some vehement in their condemnation of a supposed suspect, and some allow poetic licence to run away with them. What they have done is create a story that gets better for the telling. The writers have made a legend.

I cannot offer you an absolutely positive answer to the question 'Who was Jack the Ripper?' and nor can anyone else, however convinced they may be in their own mind that they have discovered the final solution. Here is a little of the cornucopia of facts about the case, and if your interest is stimulated you too can progress to reading all the books and material evidence available and when you have analysed it you will come to your own conclusions, or possibly a brand new theory. You will then have joined that international band of people, who like to refer to themselves as 'Ripperologists'.

The Victims

It was Friday 31 August 1888, at about quarter to four in the morning, when George Cross, a carman, walking along Bucks Row, Whitechapel, on his way to work, saw lying on the pavement on the opposite side of the road what appeared to be the lifeless body of a woman. He crossed over to have a closer look, and was joined by John Paul, a market porter, who had been walking behind him. Finding that the woman's face and hands were cold, and thinking that she was just suffering from an excess of drink, they decided to leave her and seek the help of a policeman. A few moments later PC 97J Neil, patrolling his beat, also came across the body. He signalled with his lamp for help and was soon joined by PC 96J Thain from the adjoining beat. They directed the feeble light of their bull lamps on to the inert figure, and saw what was only too obvious: she was dead. The body was on its back, with the head inclined to one side, the eyes opened wide in a sightless stare. Blood trickled from a deep gash in the throat. Thain immediately went for assistance, and Dr Llewellyn, a police surgeon who lived locally, in the Whitechapel Road, promptly attended the scene. Having examined the body, he pronounced the woman dead and ordered her removal to the public mortuary in Old Montague Street. She was placed on a hand ambulance and wheeled away. All that remained at the scene was a tiny pool of blood.

The woman was identified as Mary Ann Nichols, or Polly Nichols as she was known in and around the Whitechapel district. Cross had found the first Ripper victim. She was not to be the last.

Just over a week later, on Saturday 8 September, shortly after six o'clock in the morning, old John Davis came out of the dingy room that he occupied in a rundown lodging house at 29, Hanbury Street, and stepped into the narrow enclosed passage that ran along the side of the house from the front to the back. Standing on top of the three stone steps that led into the back yard he looked down and saw lying outstretched on the ground to his left, between the steps and the dividing fence, the body of a woman. She lay on her back, with her legs wide apart, her knees drawn up, and her feet flat on the ground. Her throat had been viciously cut right back to the spine, and the abdomen had been slashed open causing the viscera to spill out. There were coins – two new farthings laid out between her legs, and on the ground above her head there was an envelope bearing the seal of the Sussex Regiment on the flap. There was no address, only the letter 'M' and a postmark, 'London 28 August 1888'. Elsewhere in the yard, there was a leather apron, soaking in a bucket of water.

Inspector Joseph Chandler from Commercial Street Station was first on the scene. He took the necessary details, then called Dr George Bagster Phillips, the Divisional Surgeon, to examine the body. He made some notes, and by 7am the body had been removed from the scene to the mortuary.

The woman was identified as Annie Chapman, known as 'Dark Annie'. The Ripper had found and disposed of his second victim.

★

It was 12.45am and James Brown, a boxmaker, was on his way to get something to eat. As he walked along Berner Street, he saw a man and a woman standing by the wall of the Board School. The man was dressed in a long coat and was leaning over the woman, supporting himself against the wall with one hand and talking in a low tone. As Brown passed he heard her say, 'Not tonight, some other night.'

Louis Diemschutz, driving his horse and trap, was making his way home in the early hours of the morning. He had been at market all day selling cheap jewellery, and as he turned into the entrance of the unlit court that led from Berner Street into Dutfields Yard, his horse reared up in the traces and stopped. He tried to get it to walk on but it refused. He peered into the darkness to see what was causing the problem and made out the shape of what he later described as a 'little heap', which he thought might be some mud. 'I touched the heap with the handle of my whip, and then I found it was not mud. I jumped off the trap and struck a match. When I saw that it was the body of a woman, I ran indoors.'

He ran into the International Working Men's Educational Club, where he acted as steward, and returning with a lamp, looked at what had caused his horse to shy. It was the body of a tall woman, dressed in black. She lay on her back with her right hand across her chest, the dead fingers tightly clutching a paper twist of cachous. There was a deep incision in her neck which commenced 2½ inches below the left side of her jaw and terminated on the right side 1½ inches below the jawline. The carotid artery on the left side was partially cut causing the blood to flow freely, and the trachea had been completely severed. When found she was still warm and her clothing had not been disarranged. The police were informed and again Dr Bagster Phillips was called out. This time after his examination, he decided to examine the hands and clothing of all the members of the club for blood. It was five o'clock in the morning before he finished and the police left the scene.

The body was that of a Swedish woman named Elizabeth Stride, or 'Long Liz'. On Sunday 30 September, the Ripper had struck again. She was not going to be his only victim on that cold windy night. But had hungry James Brown been the first person to see Jack the Ripper?

It was exactly one o'clock in the morning when Catherine Eddowes walked out of the front door of Bishopsgate Police Station. She had been arrested for being drunk and incapable earlier that evening, and having spent four and a half hours in a cell sobering up had been released.

It was forty-four minutes later when PC 881 Watkins, patrolling his beat, walked into Mitre Square, and saw lying on the pavement in a pool of blood the body of a woman. She, like the others, lay on her back, her abdomen and chest ripped open and her face slashed. When examined by the police surgeon, it was found that one of her kidneys was missing. The woman, who less than an hour previously had left the safe custody of a police cell, had been killed in a most horrendous manner. It was less than an hour since Jack the Ripper had claimed his third victim. He had now found his fourth.

October passed by without a Ripper-style murder, and there was a general lessening of tension in and around the Whitechapel area. The local prostitutes again plied their services on the sad streets of that part of Victorian London. There was a sense of carnival in the air, for Friday 9 November was the day when the citizens of London could immerse themselves in the processional spectacle of the inauguration of Sir James Whitehead as their new Lord Mayor. The day dawned damp and overcast, and at about midday a buzz went round the waiting crowds. It was rumoured that there had been another Ripper victim. That morning John McCarthy, the owner of Miller Court – a tiny little enclave of rented rooms off Dorset Street – had become impatient about the non-payment of rent for number 13, so he sent Thomas Bowyer, his young assistant, to collect his dues. Knocking on the door and receiving no reply, Bowyer went to the room's only window; putting his hand through a broken pane of glass, he pulled aside the tattered curtain and looked in. He was the first person to see the most appalling of the Ripper victims. The newspapers of the time refused to report fully what Dr Bond found when he first saw her; however notes of his examination were most revealing.

'She was lying naked in the middle of the bed, the shoulders flat, but the axis of the body inclined to the left side of the bed. The head was turned on the left cheek. The left arm was close to the body with the forearm flexed at a right angle, and lying across the abdomen. The right arm was slightly abducted from the body, and rested on the mattress, the elbow bent and the forearm supine, with fingers clenched. The legs were wide apart, the left thigh at right angles to the trunk and the right forming an obtuse angle with the pubis.

The whole of the surface of the abdomen and thighs was removed and the abdominal cavity emptied of its viscera. The breasts were cut off, the arms mutilated by several jagged wounds, and the face hacked beyond recognition of the features. The tissues of the neck were severed all round, down to the bone.

The viscera were found in various parts, viz: the uterus and kidneys with one breast under the head, the other breast by the right foot, the liver between the feet, the intestines by the right side, and the spleen by the left side of the body. The flaps removed from the abdomen and thighs were on the table.'

This graphic medical description said it all. Bowyer had found Mary Jane Kelly, Jack the Ripper's fifth and final victim.

These were the five women that police at the time believed were victims of the Ripper, and whose deaths were investigated in the ensuing inquiry; but the list does not end there.

There were a number of other women who were murdered either before or after these killings. These murders were investigated by the police but were not subsequently considered to be part of the Ripper series. The other names have been drawn into the mystery by persons who argue vociferously about the number of victims of this sadistic killer, and which over the years have only succeeded in confusing the issue.

It is the majority view that there were only five Ripper victims. Is it possible there were more?

Other Supposed Victims

As stated above, a number of murders perpetrated at the time of the Ripper killings were purported to be the work of the same man but it should be remembered that these victims were not murdered in the same manner as the others, and although some of them are included in police files, they were placed there because they were classified as being possible rather than potential victims. They were investigated and excluded from the Ripper series.

Elizabeth Smith
On 3 April 1888 in Osborn Street, prostitute Emma Elizabeth Smith, who had a reputation for extreme violence when she was drunk, was savagely assaulted, raped and a blunt instrument forced into her lower abdomen, tearing her perineum. She was taken to the London Hospital where she died of peritonitis. Before she succumbed, she gave a description of the gang who had attacked her, yet no one thought of telling the police until three days later, when the coroner held the inquest. Some descriptive material on this case can be found in the Ripper file, and although it was investigated this murder was never considered to be one of the series.

Martha Tabrum

The body of Martha Tabrum was found on 7 August 1888, in the early hours of the morning, on the first-floor landing of George Yard Buildings. She had been stabbed thirty-nine times all over her body. The investigation into this murder led police to believe that it had been committed by a soldier, and identification parades were held at the Tower of London and at Wellington Barracks. Two men were picked out, but both had alibis for the time in question. The coroner's inquest concluded that death was due to murder by persons unknown. Again, this is another case which can be found in the official Ripper file at the Public Record Office, but because of the different method of killing, i.e. by numerous stabs in the body, probably with a bayonet, it was not considered to be one of the Ripper murders.

Alice McKenzie ('Clay Pipe Alice')

Another murder that was associated with the Ripper series and is also included in the police file, was the murder of Alice McKenzie, known as 'Clay Pipe Alice'. She was found in Castle Alley on 17 July 1889. The body like the others was described as lying in a pool of blood, and was still warm when discovered by PC 272 'H' Andrews while working his beat.

Examination of the body revealed that there were stab wounds in the throat which had caused death, and superficial stab wounds in the body that had been made after death. This was hardly a killing with the same ferocity that was the hallmark of Jack the Ripper, whose means of dispatching his victims had always been deep cuts in the throat and plunging incisions in the lower abdomen and chest.

One interesting aspect of this murder was that the first examination of the body was carried out by Dr Bagster Phillips, who had examined other Ripper victims, but Robert Anderson, the Assistant Commissioner in charge of the CID, was not, it seems, entirely satisfied, and asked for a second examination to be made by Dr Bond. There is no doubt that this request was made to satisfy Anderson that this was not a resurgence of the same series of crimes which he believed had stopped after the death of Kelly. It was a wise precaution in view of the criticism that he had been subjected to during the Ripper inquiry. Knowledgeable medical opinion from *two* eminent doctors who had been personally involved in the examination of some of the five victims during the previous year would provide a good riposte to any suggestions that this was one of the same series, and that the police had not in fact resolved the Ripper case.

Annie Farmer

There was an incident on 21 November 1888 when a woman named Annie Farmer claimed she was attacked in Satchell's Lodging House at 19, George Street. Screams were heard coming from the kitchen, and when other residents rushed down to see what the noise was about, Farmer alleged that a man had attacked her and then rushed out of the house. They checked outside, but there was no sign of him. Her only injury was a slight cut to the throat and it was generally believed that it was self-inflicted.

Rose Mylett

On 20 December 1888 the body of Rose Mylett was found in Clarke's Yard, off Poplar High Street. She was thought to have been strangled but Sir Robert Anderson in his autobiography maintains she died of natural causes. However, it was another name added to the endless list of murdered women who were believed to be Ripper victims, when in fact there was very little to connect them with the Ripper's *modus operandi*. Such was the euphoria created by the press of the time.

Unidentified trunk of a woman

Another of these supposed victims was an unidentified woman whose trunk was found under the railway arches in Pinchin Street on 10 September 1889. Although it is one of

the cases in the police file, it has little to recommend it as one
of the Ripper murders. Dismemberment, while horrific, was
not the same as the savage incisions in the neck and abdomen
that were the hallmark of the Ripper.

Francis Coles ('Carroty Nell')
On 13 February 1891, Frances Coles was found in Swallow
Gardens, murdered in a manner similar to the familiar Ripper
method, i.e. cutting of the throat and ripping of the lower
abdomen. This is a murder which although suggestive of the
Ripper's style must be eliminated because it is outside the
time period for that series of killings.

So Who Was It?

The police and Home Office files on Jack the Ripper are kept
in the Public Record Office at Kew, where they can be drawn
and inspected by whoever is interested. The material in the
police files is disappointing for it contains very little in the
way of statements and factual reports.

When Scotland Yard was based in the Embankment building, the filing systems there were in the form of endless
shelves and racks. When the racks were filled the early
records were removed and more recent ones took their place.
The old records were stored in a convenient cellar, where
they mouldered until ultimately destroyed.

This system has led to the belief that important papers in
the files have been deliberately removed to protect someone
of importance. This is just not true. There is no doubt that
papers have been removed over the years, many of them by
over-enthusiastic and avaricious readers and researchers – in
fact, one of the most important documents from the Ripper
file is today in private hands. I have spoken to many police
officers over the years and although they were not associated
with the Ripper case, there has never been a hint or a whisper
that papers had been taken from the files as a cover-up. There

is no doubt in my mind that if there had been a cover-up, then there would be *some* knowledge retained within the Force as to the reasons for such action, and it would have filtered down by word of mouth.

Also there were the problems caused by bombing during the Second World War when the Yard received a number of direct hits, which destroyed many files. Some years ago a retired police officer who had been working at the Yard during those trying times, told me that after the bombings the papers which were salvaged were sometimes only the partial remnants of the original files, added to which problem were difficulties of trying to identify thousands of pieces of disassociated paper.

However, there are certain documents which give a possible indication about the identity of the killer. The McNaughton notes in the file do indicate the three main suspects – Druitt, Kosminsky, and Ostrog – and there is a good chance that the Ripper was one of these three. Why? you may ask. Well, there are a number of very important reasons for this supposition. If you were to open a file of an unsolved crime today, you would find among the statements and reports, objective notes made by the detective in charge of the investigation, stating who in his/her opinion was the most likely suspect. However, it is one thing to know who has committed a crime, it is another matter to prove it. Lack of hard proof has prevented many cases from being finally resolved.

When McNaughton made his notes they were written as a reply to the *Sun* newspaper, who were alleging that a man called Cutbush was the Ripper. McNaughton was identifying those people any one of which could have been the Ripper working from information that was available to him as the senior officer of the detective force. It is likely that he, with a number of others, *knew* who Jack the Ripper was, but the Victorian ethic of keeping quiet unless there was a successful prosecution, prevented them from making the knowledge public. Little has changed. If a person is charged and the prosecution fails, it does not necessarily mean that the person who has walked free is innocent. It means that in many cases he has been represented by a more articulate defence counsel than the one employed by the Crown.

The Suspects

There is no shortage of books and articles concerning the identity of Jack the Ripper. Ripperology has become a million-dollar industry, and this series of murders in 1888 has become the subject of international interest. Inquiries into the case are endless, and dozens of books, films, plays, television and radio programmes have used it as a focal theme. There have been hundreds of ideas published, complete with each writer's positive proof of the identity of this serial killer. Yet when I am asked who the murderer was, I have to say I do not know for certain, and nor does anyone else. What I can say is that I know who was the most likely suspect. When I respond in this negative manner, it is often assumed that as I am speaking as the ex-Curator of the Crime Museum and the Yard's crime historian, I have access to all the criminal records, and that I am deliberately concealing the truth. I do not have access to all the records unless they are of historical significance, and the case is many years old. There are not hidden away in the cellars of the Yard secret documents which are deliberately suppressed because they will reveal some scandal, involving public figures of the period, and whose social status precludes police from revealing the real identity of the killer.

From this plethora of created doubt have evolved some of the most ludicrous and mind-stretching theories imaginable, and it would serve us well to determine how all this developed, and bring some practical common sense back to what has become a farcical situation.

Why does this case capture the public imagination so thoroughly? The primary reason lies in the fact that it is the first recorded instance of multiple sex murders, and the second reason is the period and the place where the events occurred: Victorian London. The minds of Ripperology enthusiasts are stimulated into imaginings of men in top hats, wearing long black coats, carrying black Gladstone bags containing long knives, wandering around London's fog-bound, gaslit streets picking up young prostitutes in order to satisfy their homicidal lusts by killing them. Nothing is further from the truth.

The following paragraphs describe some of the named suspects and the people who identified them.

R. J. Lees

This man was a Victorian spiritualist and clairvoyant who had a number of visions and premonitions of the Ripper murders. He was convinced that he had psychically identified the Ripper and when he saw a man boarding a bus at Shepherd's Bush, followed him to his house in the West End where he tried to have him arrested. He recorded in his diary that he had offered his services to the police but they declined to take advantage of the offer. Lees visualised seventeen murders, which even in Victorian London was, to say the least, a little extreme. Evidence available shows that his association with the case was tenuous and the product of writer's imaginative interpretation rather than fact.

Jack Pizer

This man was a boot finisher and well-known around the Whitechapel area as 'Leather Apron'. He was immediately suspected by the local residents of being the Ripper when the leather apron found in the yard after the murder of Annie Chapman was assumed to be his. This illustrates the negative quality of supposition. The immediate assumption in the minds of those feeding on malicious gossip, exaggerated out of all proportion to the facts, allowed the lynch mobs to gather and hunt for the person who they thought was guilty of the crimes. They would find a scapegoat at all costs, if only to justify their ignorance. Pizer was fortunately located by the police first, at a house where he was being hidden by friends.

After questioning he was released because the investigating officers were sure that he was not involved in the Ripper murders.

Dr Neill Cream

Cream's reputation as one of the Ripper suspects comes from the man who hanged him in 1892 for murdering a number of prostitutes by poisoning them.

The hangman is alleged to have sworn to the fact that as he dropped, Cream's last words were, 'I am Jack the . . .' What is certain about this man is that he was at the time of the Ripper murders safely imprisoned in the Illinois State Penitentiary at Joliet, near Chicago in America. Suggestions that he had bribed his way out of prison, and that his handwriting was the same as the Ripper's, are again more imaginative than objective.

The Duke of Clarence

The royal connection and the idea that the Duke of Clarence was the Ripper have become firmly embedded in the minds of many people. This fatuous plot is outlined by Stephen Knight in his book *The Final Solution* where he makes a connection between the Duke of Clarence and a woman called Annie Elizabeth Crook, to whom he is allegedly secretly married. The marriage is purportedly witnessed by the Victorian artist Walter Sickert and one of the victims, Mary Jane Kelly. As Knight progresses with his story line, we discover that there are in fact two others – Sir William Gull, the Queen's Surgeon, and a coachman called John Netley – who are involved a plot with Sir Robert Anderson, the head of the CID . . . They drive around Whitechapel in the dead of night, clattering through the cobbled streets, killing a number of prostitutes in their search to find the witness to the Duke's alleged marriage to Crook. They finally find Kelly in Miller Court where they dispose of her in a most gruesome fashion, by cutting up the body .

Stephen Knight created an enormous myth when he

wrote his book, mainly from the fantasies of a man called Joseph Sickert who claimed that he was the son of Walter Sickert. Joseph later admitted that what he had told Knight was a lie. Sadly Knight was quite aware of what he was doing. In creating a novel of fact and fiction, he added more hyperbole to the Ripper legend. People to whom he spoke while researching his narrative told him that many of his central facts were untrue, yet he continued to perpetrate the deception.

The focal point of his argument lies with Annie Elizabeth Crook's allegedly secret marriage to the Duke of Clarence. To make the story more convincing he identifies Crook as having a child by the Duke, supporting it with a birth certificate showing that she gave birth to a girl in 1885. He compounds the myth by implying that she was the same person as a woman called Elizabeth Cook who lived at 6, Cleveland Street, an area frequented by the Duke. Here we have one of the classic role models for the Ripper: a member of the Royal family.

Frederick Bailey Deeming

The death mask of this man can be seen in the museum, and the responsibility for him being identified as Jack the Ripper can probably be laid at the feet of previous incumbents of the post of Curator of the Museum.

Deeming had killed his wife and children at Rainhill near Liverpool, and buried them under the hearth. He then emigrated to Melbourne in Australia with his second wife, and within a short time he murdered her. He was tried and found guilty of murder and subsequently hanged. After death his body was dissected in order to determine whether any of his organs had degenerated, because there was a current belief that if you were a criminal then your body would degenerate internally.

This was the classic sort of naive criminology that existed at the time. What would they have done if they had found that Deeming's organs had degenerated? Open up everyone arrested to see whether their physical condition was such that they could be identified as criminals, and add the fact to any evidence they had?

The Available Evidence

So who was this mystery killer who terrorised Whitechapel and who has been the focus of constant attention by writers, and what evidence is there to aid identification of the Ripper?

There are three important documents, to consider. First there are the McNaughton notes, written by the Assistant Commissioner of Police where he names Dr Ostrog, Montague Druitt, and a man called Kosminsky. Is it possible that the Ripper was one of these three? Even these notes have been called into doubt. There are two sets. One in the file, and another that was in the possession of Lady Aberconway who was Sir Melvin McNaughton's daughter. Perusal of these notes by two writers led to the identification of Montague Druitt as the most likely candidate. There was positive evidence implicating him, and I believed that he was the most likely suspect until new papers came to light in 1988, the centenary of the murders.

Often when the files of unsolved cases are looked at, one finds notes as to whom the detective in charge of the inquiry believed to be responsible for committing the crime. But although there may be the strongest reasons for believing that one particular suspect is responsible for the crime under investigation, it is necessary to provide the evidence to prove it in a court of law. If that evidence is not forthcoming then the case must remain open.

This is the simple answer as to why the Ripper murders have remained unsolved. Although the Police possibly iden-tified the murderer it was just not possible to arrest him because there was insufficient evidence to convict him. All the theorising in the world is not going to reveal who he was, until there is some hard proof.

The other two documents concerning the identity of the Ripper are in private hands. One of them is an official document from the original police file and should be housed with the rest of the available papers in the Public Record Office, but unless they are surrendered voluntarily there is little that can be done.

The first of these documents is a memo written by the Assistant Commissioner Sir Robert Anderson to Superintendent Williamson who was in charge of the CID at the time of the murders. It reads as follows:

I am convinced that the Whitechapel murder case is one which can be successfully grappled with if it is systematically taken in hand. I go so far as to say, that I could myself in a few days unravel the mystery, provided I could spare the time and give undivided attention to it. I feel therefore the utmost importance to be attached to putting the whole Central Office work in this case in the hands of one man , who will have nothing else to concern himself with. Neither you or I Mr Williamson can do this. I therefore put it in the hands of Chief Inspector Swanson who must be acquainted with every detail. I look upon him for the time being as the eyes and ears of the Commissioner in this particular case.

He must have a room to himself, and every paper, every document, every report, every telegram, must pass through his hands. He must be consulted on every subject. I would not send any directions anywhere on the subject of the murder without consulting him. I give him the whole responsibility. On the other hand he should consult you Mr Williamson, or myself, on every important particular before any action unless there is some extreme urgency.

I find that a most important letter was sent to . . . yesterday without his seeing it . This is quite an error and should not occur again. All the papers in Central Office on the subject of the murder, must be kept in his room, and plans of the positions etc.

I must have this matter at once put on a proper footing, so as to be a guide for the future in cases of importance.

Everything depends upon a careful compliance with these directions.

Although the memo is not dated, Williamson added a minute which is initialled and signed 12 September 1888. The minute is not easy to decipher, but relates to the passing of letters received directly to Swanson: 'Every document, letter, received in . . . on this subject should go to his room upon being docketed, and he should . . . forthwith for it being docketed when necessary.'

The date of this minute shows that it was written after the second murder, and it shows that Chief Inspector Swanson was in charge of the case and not Inspector Abberline, as was believed for many years.

This is important when referring to the third piece of evidence. This can be found in a book called *The Lighter Side of My Official Life* written by Sir Robert Anderson. On page 138 where he refers to the Ripper murders, he tells the reader that

'undiscovered murders are rare in London, and the Jack the Ripper crimes are not within that category. If the police here had powers such as the French Police possess, the murderer would have been brought to justice. Scotland Yard can boast that not even the subordinate officers of the department will tell tales out of school, and it would ill become me to violate the unwritten rule of the service. So I will only add here that the Jack the Ripper letter which is preserved at New Scotland Yard is the creation of an enterprising London journalist'. This is immediately followed by a handwritten note by Swanson, 'Known to Scotland Yard head officers of CID.'

The letter referred to was one received at the Central News Agency dated 25 September 1888.

Anderson continues, 'Having regard to the interest attaching to this case, I am almost tempted to disclose the identity of the murderer and of the pressman who wrote the letter above referred to. But no public benefit would result from such a course and the traditions of my old department would suffer.' This last sentence must be the understatement of the century. Everyone would have benefited a great deal if he had revealed all. He continues, 'I will merely add that the only person who had ever had a good view of the murderer unhesitatingly identified the suspect the instant he was confronted with him; but he refused to give evidence against him.' This is followed by more handwritten notes from Swanson: 'because the suspect was also a Jew, and also because the evidence would convict the suspect, and witness would be the means of the murderer being hanged, which he did not wish to be left on his mind'. This is followed by Swanson's initials *D.S.S.* In the margin he writes another comment, 'and after this identification which suspect knew, no other murder of this kind took place in London.'

Swanson's comments do not end here. On one of the blank leaves at the end of the book Swanson writes again in his own hand.

'continuing from page 138, after the suspect had been identified at the Seaside Home where he had been sent by us with difficulty, in order to subject him to identification, and he knew he was identified. On suspects return to his brothers house in Whitechapel he was watched by police(City CID) by day and night. In a very short time the suspect with his hands tied behind his back, he was sent to Stepney Workhouse and then to Colney Hatch and died shortly afterwards. Kosminski was the suspect.'

It was again initialled D.S.S.

The finding of these papers immediately triggered a spate of analytical journalism both for and against its factuality, and also some excellent research in trying to determine how accurate the marginal notes were. In 1888 there is no record of a Seaside Home where police officers who had been injured were sent to convalesce. The first time we know of a home for this purpose was when one was set up in 1890. A police officer who had been long retired said he had a recollection of there being one in Bexhill. There certainly was one in Brighton until recent years, and although one television programme claimed to have found evidence of an unnamed man being taken to a seaside home in Brighton, I personally have never seen any proof of this fact, or exactly where the home was located. Could it have been the same building that was purchased in Brighton to be used as the convalescent home in 1890, or was it a building miles away in Bexhill? Certainly there is no police record in existence to tell us exactly where or whether a home existed prior to 1890. Although medical services in those days were not what they are today, police have always ensured that officers injured in the course of their duty had some recourse to medical care, and there is little doubt that there was a home where police officers could recuperate after illness.

Swanson's naming of Kosminsky as the Ripper resulted in more interesting research and it was discovered that an Aaron Kosminski, a Polish Jewish hairdresser with a history of mental instability, had been admitted to various institutions both before and after the murders were committed. He died in Leavesden Asylum for Imbeciles in 1919. Was this man who was twenty-three at the time of the murders the Jack the Ripper, or was it a man named Nathan Kaminsky, or another named Aaron Cohen? It was suggested by one writer they were one and the same person. Had Swanson made an error when writing down the name ?

Kaminsky, a bootmaker, had lived in Whitechapel at the time of the murders and was known to have been treated in hospital for syphilis. Little else was known about him. Cohen was a violent man who also lived in the area. He had been confined in Colney Hatch in 1888 where he had been physically restrained because of his violent condition. He had died a year later. Reactions to these handwritten notes have caused comment and discussion. The question remains – would Swanson, the person who was definitely in charge of the inquiry and who became the first head of the murder squad, make comments that were untrue. It is possible but unlikely. However poorly they were grammatically composed, or however much criticism is levelled against them, they remain a convincing identification of the Ripper by someone directly involved with solving the case.

Kosminsky is as likely as any other to be the suspect in the absence of more positive evidence.

In 1988, on the centenary of the Ripper murder, I received an envelope which contained papers from the Ripper files that had not been seen for many years, including the original 'Dear Boss' letter. They were sent from Croydon, and the envelope was tested for fingerprints. After eliminating the prints of those who had handled it, one set was found of which there was no trace. Who sent them has never been discovered. I also found other interesting material relating to the Ripper. While going through some old photograph albums that had been used for CID training, I found pictures of the five victims. The scramble to release them to the press was one of the most remarkable experiences of my forty years with the Metropolitan Police. The mystery continues. Recently I acquired a silk screen printed shawl. It had been in the donor's family for years and a large section has been cut out reputedly by his mother, because she did not like the blood stains on it. I am told that it was the shawl worn by Catherine Eddowes when she was killed. Who knows what will come to light next?

8

MILSOM AND FOWLER

There is a corner of the museum where visitors can see a number of hanging ropes. They show the types of rope that were used in the early part of the eighteenth century, and are examples of the different quality of cordage used by the hangman until the abolition of the death penalty in 1969. The early ropes were made of just four thin strands of sisal, which ran through a small metal eyelet to form the noose. Later patterns were much heavier and comprised mixtures of different rope materials. The last type to be used in an execution was made from eight strands of Italian hemp, with a large moulded brass thimble to take the thicker rope. The noose was covered with leather which was greased with Vaseline to stop it burning the neck. Three of the ropes in the museum collection have a special significance, for they were all used at the same time – when three murderers were hanged together on the scaffold at Newgate.

Albert Milsom and Henry Fowler selected a dilapidated run-down residence, standing in its own grounds at Tetherdown, Fortis Green, as their target for getting money. It was owned by a retired engineer, Henry Smith, who was rather an

eccentric old man, living alone with just the help of a gardener-cum-odd-job man. To the two ex-convicts it looked an
easy   take – a large remote house occupied solely by a sev-
enty-nine-year-old man.

Late on the night of Tuesday 14 February 1896, they
climbed quietly over a locked gate, and entered the grounds.
As they stalked silently through the shrubbery towards the
house, Fowler suddenly grabbed Milsom by the arm and
pointed at the ground where in the half-light they could see a
wire stretched across their path. Gingerly they stepped over it,
thinking that it was attached to some form of alarm bell. Just
as well, for what they did not realise was that the eccentric old
Mr Smith, with the help of his gardener, had not only set up
wires to trigger alarm bells, but also some that would fire
guns should any unwanted visitors decide to make a call.

The last public hanging in England took place on 26 May
1868 outside Newgate Prison in London. Michael Barrett
was hanged for the murder of twelve people who were
killed when he exploded a bomb outside the Clerkenwell
House of Correction in an attempt to release a man
called Byrne, a member of his Fenian gang.

Carefully they approached the lawn that ran around the
house, and as there was a light in one of the upstairs rooms,
they crouched behind some shrubs to wait until everything
was in darkness and to see where would be the easiest place
to gain entry. They stayed there for over an hour whispering
and watching, and then bent double, ran silently across the
lawn towards the drawing-room window. Fowler tried to prise
it open, but it would not give. He then moved to a smaller
window, which he opened, but found there were bars across
it, making it impossible to climb through. Creeping noise-

lessly round the house they came to the kitchen window, where the sill was covered with flower pots. Quietly they lifted them off. Fowler inserted his chisel into the jamb and applied pressure. There was a sharp crack as the lock broke. Gently sliding the window up, they climbed in. Milsom struck a match, and lit the small lamp he was carrying, and by its faint glow they started to look around. Suddenly they froze. There was the almost imperceptible sound of someone walking around upstairs. A faint light appeared through the keyhole and under the foot of the kitchen door. The light got stronger and as the intruders waited, the footsteps paused. The light shining through the keyhole went out, and they heard the sound of a key being turned in the lock. As the door slowly opened, they could see silhouetted against the frame, the outline of the old man, leaning curiously forward to see what had disturbed his sleep. As he entered the room, they both leapt on top of him, knocking him down on to the cold hard tiled floor. When he started to shout, they began to beat him mercilessly on the head with the small clubs they were carrying. Slowly the old man sank into unconsciousness whereupon the intruders tied him up. In the light coming from the hallway they could see that Mr Smith was bleeding profusely from the wounds to his head, and was having difficulty breathing. They made an attempt to stem the blood, by cutting a kitchen towel into strips with their penknives, then wrapping them around his head, but to no avail. He was dying.

They rummaged through the pockets of his dressing gown and finding a key, started to search the house. Upstairs in the old man's bedroom they found what they were looking for – a safe. Opening it, they saw the money they had come to get. Pocketing it, they left by the way they had entered, stopping only to bury their tools in one of the flowerbeds. Tucked into Fowler's pocket was the result of the night's work: two white engraved Bank of England five-pound notes.

In the morning Charlie Webber, the gardener-cum-odd-job man, found his employer where the burglars had left him, lying on the kitchen floor in a pool of blood. His hands were tied behind his back with strips of tablecloth, and pieces of rag had been pushed into his mouth to silence him. Detective Inspector Nutkins from Albany Street wasted no time in attending the scene. He called the Divisional Surgeon to examine the body, and was told death was due to multiple skull fractures caused by a number of extremely vicious blows, probably with something small and heavy – something similar to a life preserver. Life preservers were coshes made of a piece of cane about 10 inches long, with bulbs of lead at both ends. They were usually covered in leather or woven cane and were often carried by people in Victorian times, to protect themselves against attack by muggers.

From the beginning it seemed likely that two men were involved, as two penknives had been found at the scene. With them was a child's toy bull lamp, a miniature of the type carried by policemen.

Detective Chief Inspector Marshall, from Scotland Yard's murder squad, was called to the scene, and with Inspector Nutkins, started to organise the investigation. Local inquiries brought to light the fact that two men had been seen prowling around in the vicinity prior to the murder. One of them, Milsom, an habitual criminal with a long list of offences behind him, had recently been released on licence, from Pentonville. By chance he was being kept under casual observation by a young trainee detective who, knowing he was a 'ticket of leave' man, made it his business to keep an eye on him, just in case he reverted to dishonesty. Milsom was known to be associating with another man with a long criminal record, Henry Fowler, who had also just been released from prison. A search for them proved fruitless: strange that they had both disappeared from the usual places they patronised, on the morning following the murder. A visit was paid to Milsom's address at 133, Southam Street, King's Cross, by Marshall and Nutkins, ostensibly to find out why he had failed to report according to the terms of his parole. They were greeted at the door by young fifteen-year-old Henry

Miller, Milsom's brother-in-law. Although Mrs Milsom was not too happy to see them, she invited them in. She was extremely irritable, and told them she had not seen her husband since Thursday, didn't know where he was, and could they hurry up and leave as she was busy. Her impatience made the two detectives realise it was pretty certain she *did* know her husband's whereabouts, but she had no intention of telling the police. Looking round, Marshall noticed what appeared to be part of a tartan dress lying on the table. What was even more interesting to him, was that the tartan material was the same as the wick in the child's bull lamp, found beside Smith's body. When they produced the lamp, young Henry fell over himself to explain that some marks on it had been made by him, and that it was definitely his lamp. Nothing was to be gained by further questioning so they left, taking a piece of the tartan material with them. As the door closed behind them, they heard the boy yelp, as Mrs Milsom boxed his ears.

On Thursday 17 May 1832, James Conner was sentenced to transportation for seven years, for the theft of a handkerchief valued at four shillings. He was twelve years old.

As the two suspects had obviously left the area, it now became a case of waiting and monitoring any information that came the way of the police. Descriptions were circulated, and a watch was kept on the families. Information came in about the offenders being seen in Swindon, then in Liverpool, next in Cardiff, and in Manchester. All were investigated. All proved cold leads.

Mrs Milsom was seen to leave her home and although discreetly followed, she managed to lose her tail. She did not return for nearly a week. It transpired later that Milsom had returned to London, and she had gone to see him.

Marshall became more determined than ever to find his suspects. The break came with a letter. A check was kept on any mail delivered to the Milsoms and on 4 April a letter was delivered with a Bath postmark. On the off-chance the two policemen went to Bath where they contacted the constabulary there and had descriptions of the two suspects circulated to local informants. Then they sat back and waited.

Their luck was in. On the morning of Sunday 12 April armed police surrounded a shop in Monmouth Street. Milsom and Fowler were seen walking down the street and as they went into the shop Marshall and Nutkins, walked in behind them. When they announced who they were, and why they were there, a fight started. Milsom came quietly, but Fowler, a bear of a man, erupted when they went to put the handcuffs on him. Some sharp taps on the head with the butt of a revolver soon reduced his resistance to arrest. Both men were hauled off to the police station, where they were kept until arrangements had been made to transfer them to London. When questioned, they blamed each other for the killing. They were subsequently charged with 'the wilful murder of Henry Smith, on or about 14 February, at Muswell Lodge . . .' together with other offences.

The trial at the Old Bailey lasted three days, during which time the evidence presented against them gave little room for doubt in the minds of the jury. When they retired, Fowler leapt across the dock and tried to strangle Milsom. The court was in an uproar for over ten minutes while he fought the warders and police who tried to restrain him. During this time the glass around the dock was smashed, chairs were broken, and there were a lot of cuts and bruises on those who had tried to subdue him. The jury returned and the foreman announced their findings: both guilty on all counts. The judge, Mr Justice Hawkins, put on his black cap, pronounced the sentence of death, and ordered Milsom and Fowler to be taken down.

There was to be one other touch of drama in the case. It was planned to hang both men on the same scaffold at the same time but because of Fowler's violence towards Milsom, it was decided that another murderer, William Seaman, should be hanged between them. As an added precaution, each prisoner would be escorted by at least four warders. When they went to the scaffold at Newgate on 9 June 1896, the execution shed was so crowded with warders and official witnesses, that Billington, the hangman, could not see that his assistant Warbrick was still tying Milsom's feet. Thinking all was ready, he pushed the lever forward. Warbrick, feeling the bolts being withdrawn, plunged into the drop holding on to the only thing he could grasp – Milsom's legs.

So ended another case of murder where the loss of human lives was just not worth the gain achieved: a mere £10.00, not a fortune even in those days. The three ropes in the museum stand as a mute witness to that, and also to the last triple hanging in this country.

9

MYTHS OF THE MUSEUM

The museum has always been the focus of a number of stories which have been told and retold and exaggerated so many times, that many people believe they are true. Whilst they may make interesting conversation pieces, they are pure myths.

The head that grows hair
This story tells of the death mask of a hanged murderer that constantly grows facial hair, to the extent that the Curator is obliged to trim and shape the beard regularly, to prevent it from becoming too long.

This ludicrous tale relates to the death mask of Heinrich Himmler, who was head of Adolf Hitler's SS. When Himmler committed suicide, a number of these masks were made, of which only three have survived. The museum has two and these were made by Chief Superintendent Burt of the Special Branch, who was in Germany after the Second World War assisting with the reorganisation of the police. To make them he used the 'Moulage Method', where a mask of latex rubber is moulded directly from the face, and this in turn is used as a female mould to make a cast of the face in plaster of Paris or wax. The museum has one in each material.

To give the wax mask realism, it was made in a flesh colour, and to increase the effect hair was added to the eyebrows and the nostrils. Some visitor, seeing this, related a story of 'the mask with hair growing on it', and so the myth grew. It has become very difficult over the years for the Curator to convince people that the story is simply not true.

The ghost

As stated earlier, during the years of the museum's existence it has been housed in a number of different locations within both the old and the new Scotland Yards. At each location there have been those who have started rumours of ghostly apparitions wandering the corridors, or eerie sounds to be heard in the vicinity of the museum.

There are two recorded spiritual visitations to the museum. The first is reported to have occurred at the Scotland Yard establishment on the Embankment. During the building's construction the naked, headless, and limbless torso of a woman was found. Later a leg and an arm were discovered, also a small silver crucifix. The find was a mystery that was never solved, the woman's identity was never determined.

Subsequently the ghost of her headless body was reported to have been seen a number of times, although apparently her limbs were intact. The second ghost story appears to have been started by a woman who was passing the entrance of the museum late at night and heard a strange noise within. She immediately rushed downstairs to the office of the Back Hall Inspector, and reported the incident. The Inspector, somewhat sceptical, went to investigate and, having listened at the door for a time and also heard the noises, decided to knock on the door. It was opened by the Curator who explained that he was working late in order to set up a new display. Let me assure the reader that there has never been a ghost in the museum, and the only apparition one is likely to see is that of a practical joker.

The bloodstained spade
This is a recent myth that has apparently evolved from some visitor putting his own interpretation on what he saw in the museum.

There is a spade in the display that was connected with the tragic murder of a young child. The blade of the tool has traces of red paint on it, and it is presumably this that the observer has assumed to be blood.

There is absolutely no truth in this story. It is the product of an over-imaginative journalist.

Spending a night in the museum
No one has ever spent a night in the museum, and left the following morning with their hair having turned white with the horror of what they have seen or heard. Nor has anyone been taken off to a mental institution after a night in the museum because it has turned their minds.

This story has been related to me a number of times, although I have never seen it in print. I even heard someone relating that he knew a person who had done it, and survived.

No one has ever been given permission to sleep in the museum, although there have been requests from various people, who would like to do it to satisfy a bet. It is not likely that such a request will ever be granted.

So if you are thinking of applying, my advice would be to save the price of the stamp and paper.

10

THE TOTTENHAM OUTRAGE

An incident occurred in 1909 that caused a hue and cry which had all the ingredients of the Keystone Cops, except there was no humour in the situation. It was the chase of two anarchists who had carried out a robbery. A young boy and a police officer were killed in the pursuit, which covered six and a half miles, and a total of twenty-five persons who joined in, were injured.

Although one can still retrace the route taken by the two villains who were the subjects of the chase, Jacob Hefeld and Paul Meyer, many of the incident sites have now been built on. All accounts of this event are based on the official report submitted by Superintendent W. Jenkins who was the officer in charge of 'N' Division. It was written during the fortnight following the incident, when he had gathered all the known facts, and is presented here in the format and layout of the original, complete with spelling mistakes and misquotes of names. It is written in the style of the time, for submission to the Commissioner, and was typed, probably by a clerk, on one of the newfangled typewriters which had recently been issued to police stations.

METROPOLITAN POLICE

Stoke Newington Station,
'H' Division
7th day of February, 1909

MURDER, ATTEMPTED MURDER, SHOOTING AND
ARREST OF THE MURDERERS
BY POLICE 'N' DIVISION

I beg to report that at 10.30am, 23rd ult., Joseph Wilson a chauffeur, age 29, of 22 West Hampstead Mews, Hampstead, accompanied by Albert Keyworth, age 17, an office boy, of 16, Seaford Road, South Tottenham, arrived at the factory of Mr Schnurmann, rubber merchant, Chestnut Road, Tottenham, in a motor car. The youth alighted carrying a canvas bag containing about £80 gold, silver and bronze, which he had brought from the London and South Western Bank, South Hackney, for the wages of the men, a weekly custom.

Two men of foreign type, named Jacob and Helfeld,, stood at the entrance of the premises, one at each side. Jacob seized the boy and the bag, and shot at him, but inflicted no injury. There was a momentary struggle; they both fell, but the man got up with the money. The chauffeur went promptly to the boy's assistance, when he was seized by Jacob. He laid hold of the bag, however, and grasped Jacob by the throat, both fell and struggled desperately. Helfeld shot at the chauffeur repeatedly, his overcoat was riddled with bullets and a slanting shot passed through every garment, including his under-vest, in the region of his stomach. In a miraculous and unaccountable way he escaped injury. The chauffeur cried loudly for help and a man named George Smith, a gas stoker, of 17, Hartington Road, Tottenham, went and gripped Jacob and threw him, the bag of money falling upon the pavement. Whilst struggling together, Smith was shot in the chest by Helfeld. Jacob released himself and took the money, at the same moment discharging his revolver into Smith. His escape from death was equally remarkable.

The assailants then ran off towards Tottenham Marshes, proceeding by way of Chestnut Grove, Scales Road and Mitchley Road.

The revolver shots were heard by Police at the Tottenham Police Station situated immediately opposite the rubber factory.

P.C.s. 403 'N' Tyler and 510 'N' Newman, who were on reserve duty, ran out. The chauffeur rapidly explained the position of things and with the latter, P.C. got in the car and followed them. P.C. Tyler pursued on foot.

P.C.s 406 'N' Bond and 637 'N' Fraiser, hearing the alarm, leaped through the open boot room window into Chustnut Road, followed by other officers who were aroused from sleep, and who hastily put on some clothing and ran out by the front entrance and took up the chase.

The car overtook the assailants at Mitchley Road, and the occupants were met with a fusillade of shots, damaging the glass windscreen, hood and radiator of the car, rendering it useless.

P.C. received a graze on the cheek and a small wound on the lobe of his right ear. A crowd of persons joined the chase, among them was Ralph Joscelyne, age 10 years, a schoolboy of 3, Rugby House, Colsterworth Road, Tottenham, who was mortally wounded by a bullet wound in the right breast. he was conveyed to Tottenham Hospital where he was found to be dead. He was subsequently identified by his mother.

After these incidents the murderers proceeded rapidly by way of the road to the Dust Destructor, situated on the marshes in a north easterly direction. Constables Tyler and Newman crossed in a northerly direction with a view to heading them off. When opposite the Dust Destructor, Tyler was approaching them from the marsh land and called upon them to surrender, but the man Helfeld, who is living, stood and took deliberate aim and shot him in the head, which proved almost immediately fatal. Constable Newman remained with his fallen comrade.

Sub-Divisional Inspector Large arrived and Tyler was carried into a house near by. An ambulance was sent for and he was conveyed with all speed to Tottenham Hospital, and five minutes after admission died.

The chase which had now become most desperate, was continued with a splendid determination. The murderers proceeded over the footbridge spanning the Great Eastern Railway, then in a north easterly direction to the west bank of the River Lea. Following the course to Chalk Bridge which spans the river just beyond the rifle butts, thence on to the Mill Stream Bridge, where they held the crowd at bay for a considerable time. It was here that P.C. 'N' Nicod went a short distance ahead of the crowd, knelt down upon the banks with a view of shooting the murderers, but the revolver (a private one) which he had, was found to be defective. Before he could beat a retreat, both miscreants fired upon him and both shots took effect. He was wounded in the calf of his left leg and thigh. Just previously a lad named Cyril Burgess of 65 Wycombe Road, Tottenham, was wounded by a bullet fired by one of the men, in the inner side of the right ankle.

The men then passed on through a footway to the south side of the Banbury Reservoir, thence northward through a narrow pathway towards Higham Hill. Here Sydney Charles Slater, aged 30, a horse keeper of 6 Eaton Place, Fore Street, Edmonton, rather recklessly followed these men into this footpath, when the murderers fired 6 or 7 shots at him. He was hit in the right thigh and disabled. First aid was rendered by Police and he was conveyed to Tottenham Hospital.

They crossed by the base of Higham Hill, through some allotments. Frederick Easter, age 27, a single man, of 1 Billet Road, Higham Hill, joined in the chase. When in Folly Lane, the murderers turned and fired upon their pursuers and Easter was shot, the bullet striking him on the left thigh and passing through the fleshy part of his left leg. They now entered a field where there was a gipsy encampment. In the same reckless way the miscreants fired amongst the gipsies, but fortunately without causing any hurt or damage. They then entered the premises of Salisbury Hall Farm and took temporary shelter behind a haystack. From either side of it they continually fired upon the pursuers who were fully exposed to the deadly fire. Many saved themselves by promptly lying down flat on the ground. It was during this severe encounter that William Roker, age 32, a labourer, of 4 Cross Street, Edmonton, was severely injured, being shot in both legs. He was promptly attended to and conveyed to the Walthamstow Cottage Hospital, where he now lies in a critical condition.

The murderers then passed through the farm yard to the Chingford road. Without a moment's hesitation they comandeered an electric tram on route to the Baker's Arms I.H. Lea Bridge Road. The driver stopped the car and rushed upstairs, leaving the conductor who was forced with the muzzle of a revolver at his head, to go to the controller and Drive them with all speed. Also at this point they were holding at bay a large crowd of pursuers. an old man named Edward Loveday, aged 63, of 2 Devonshire Villas Hall Lane, Chingford, was a passenger. He made an attempt to leave the car and was shot through the neck by one of the murderers. There was also a female passenger, but she was unhurt. Loveday is an inmate of Walthamstow Hospital and is progressing favourably.

The conductor proceeded as far as the Victory P.H., St Johns Road, where there is a loop line. He reduced speed to allow a car coming in the opposite direction to pass him, and then put on full speed to Kites Corner. By a simple but ingenious ruse, he got rid of his undesirable passengers by telling the man standing by him that the Police Station was just around the corner. This was effectual for he was directed to pull up and the men hurriedly left the car. Just here they comandeered a milk cart which was stationary. George Conyard, age 19, of rose cottage, Chingford road, who was inside a shop, seeing the horse being driven off, rushed out to stop it, but he was immediately shot down, the bullet passing through his right arm and chest. He too is in Walthamstow Hospital and progressing favourably. They drove up Farnham Avenue to Forest Road, Walthamstow. Here they were overtaken by a horse and van driven by Thomas White, Greengrocer, Chingford road, Walthamstow. One of the men pointed a revolver at White's head and he jumped off his seat which the men took possession of and drove rapidly towards Wood Street.

P.C.236 'N' Adamans comandeered a motor car and followed blowing his whistle and attracted the attention P.S. Howitt and P.C. 616 'N' Francis, on duty at Hagger Bridge. These officers made an attempt to stop them, when one of the men fired at them and the bullet passed between them and broke a glass panel of the side door of 849 Forest Road, occupied by Charles Pipe, a green-grocer.

The action of the officers diverted their course. They turned into Kingsley road, driving across waste land, to Fulbourns Road, to Wadham Road, thence into Winchester Road, where they deserted the van and ran to the River Ching. Through this part of the route Jacob was driving. Helfeld possessed both revolvers, and kept up a continuous fire upon the pursuers.

They clambered down the narrow bank of the river, and Jacob succeeded in climbing the fence that bounds it. Helfeld turned round and now that his position was hopeless, he cried out to Jacob, 'Go on save yourself, I've only got two left'. He sank upon the ground and shot himself through the head. He was seized by Police, disarmed and taken as soon as possible to Tottenham Hospital in a van requisitioned on the spot and he is now detailed there under strict Police supervision. He is progressing very favourably and in a few days will be well enough to be charged.

The first murder on a train was the killing of Mr Briggs, a bank clerk, by Franz Muller on Saturday 9 July 1864. It occurred on the North London Railway, between Fenchurch Street and Hackney Wick. Muller fled the country, but was arrested when he arrived in New York. He was brought back to stand trial, found guilty and sentenced to death. He became famous for the Muller hat which was a top hat with the crown cut off. Unfortunately the hat which Muller had cut down was taken from his victim and when he was arrested it positively identified him as being the killer.

Jacob was hotly pursued by P.C. 789 'N' Zeithing and was within a few yards of him when he turned and fired three shots at him, one of which passed over his left shoulder and entered the chest of Frederick John Mortimer, aged 38, of 18 Palmerston Road, Walthamstow, and came out at the back of him. This man had just thrown a brick at Jacob. The P.C. had a very narrow escape as one or more of the bullets passed through the lapels of his greatcoat. Mortimer is in Walthamstow Hospital and progressing very favourably.

Jacob had run on across Hale End Road into a field at the rear of Oak Cottage, Hale End, occupied by Charles Relstone, a coal porter. Here he was lost sight of by everyone but as a matter of fact he had sought shelter in this small house, consisting of four rooms and a leanto. He first ran to the front room, where judging from the amount of soot which was found lying in the room, he had made an attempt to climb into the chimney. I may say that on entering the kitchen of this house, he had peered through a small window in the door of the leanto, his face was covered with blood, no doubt caused by the small shot from the fowling pieces of men who had shot at him when crossing the fields in the earlier part of the chase. Mrs Relstone saw him, screamed and ran out of the place, crying, 'Oh, my children'.

Jacob then shut and bolted the door, also the front street door. Charles Schaffer, a baker, of 22 Charlton road, Walthamstow, who had chased the men throughout, went to the door of the leanto, and with the assistance of P.C. 36 'N' Dewhurst, burst it open. Both passed into the kitchen and brought the children out safely.

After failing in his attempt to hide in the parlour chimney, Jacob went upstairs into the front bedroom, He gave a stealthy look through the window which was seen by his pursuers who had now arrived in large numbers, and some of them were armed. They at once poured a volley in the direction shattering most of the contents of the room.

At this juncture, P.C. 636 Charles Eagles, and P.C. Charles Dixon, C.I.D. 'N' and P.C. 714 John Cater rendered their service. The former obtained a ladder adjoining the premises and placed it against the back bedroom window. He obtained a loaded gun from a bystander, climbed the ladder, opened the window and looked in. P.C. Dixon had sent a dog up into this room which Eagles encouraged to go under the bed. At that moment he turned round and saw Jacob with the door of the front bedroom ajar, pointing the revolver at him. He found that the gun was unworkable through a safety catch which he did not understand, and rapidly descended the ladder. He changed the weapon for a police revolver which P.C. Dixon was carrying. The three officers then climbed this very narrow staircase, Eagles being in front, Dixon in the centre, and Cater behind. It was perfectly clear that if the miscreant secured the first shot, that these men would have been seriously hurt or killed, because it will be seen by the history of this case, that Jacob was a dead shot.

Eagles fired twice and Cater once, through the panel of the door. Now there was a shot heard in the room by most people, though these men including Eagles, assert that Jacob opened the door slightly and presented the revolver at them, but in the fearful excitement of the moment, the P.C.s could have believed this.

Evidence has since proved that a Police shot did not dispatch this man. He shot himself.

Upon Police entering the room, Jacob was found upon a small bed in the corner, in the throes of death, and immediately afterwards expired. The body was carried down into the yard and subsequently seen by Dr. Alcock of Castle Avenue, Highhams Park, and Dr. Wainwright, Surgeon, of Tottenham. It was then conveyed on a police ambulance to the Walthamstow Mortuary, Queens Road.

It has been identified as that of a Russian known as 'Yacob' who has been employed at a furniture factory at Tottenham owned by Messrs. Lebus and Company. Helfeld was formerly employed by Mr. Schnurmann, but only for a few days. Inquiries as to their antecedents are in progress by the officers of Special Branch.

In addition to the injured persons named above, the following also sustained personal injury:

William Devine, age 13, of 145 Welbourne Road, Tottenham
  Shot in the right leg.
George Harwood, age 26, of 6 Park Lane, Tottenham

Wound of forefinger right hand, inflicted at the railway bridge, supposed by Jacob as he was making his escape.

George Rawson, age 40, of 9 Havelock Road, Tottenham.
A slight bullet wound on inner side of right wrist, when the murderers were firing from the bridge spanning the Mill Stream.

Joseph Ayley, age 30 of 113 Love Lane, Tottenham

George Cousins, age 29, of 14 Aspline Road, Tottenham
Bullet in thick part of left shoulder, after lying down for a short time, resumed the chase.

William Edwards, age 28, of 4 Leeds Road, Edmonton
Received shot in the left elbow, near where P.C. Tylor fell.

P.C. 50 Hawkings
Graze over left eye and leg, but how caused is not clear. He was following the murderers in an advertisement cart. One of the murderers shot the pony, causing it to fall and Hawkings and the men with him, were thrown out. Bullets had passed through the leg and seat and leg of his trousers. He was armed with a gun but did not use it.

List of Police injured from other
causes, climbing fences etc.

P.C. Forde – sprain of left thigh.

P.C. Weadden – lacerated thumb of right hand.

P.C. Brown – jagged wound of left hand.

P.C. Bond – contracted chill through taking up the chase partly dressed.

Total number of casualties – 25.

The weapons used by these men were powerful, up to date magazines and the bullets were 'expanding'. They had but few left when captured. I am glad to say that with the exception of Roker, all the civilian patients who are of the labouring class are progressing favourably.

Upon Jacobs there were found two paper bank bags, one of which contained £5 silver, the other being empty. This would be the property of Mr Schurmann.

This extraordinary man hunt was carried over a course extending six miles.

It would be impossible for me to speak too highly of the splendid conduct of the Police of 'N' and 'J' Divisions. In response to my call to duty, they were most prompt and in action cool, tactful and fearless.

The conduct of the public engaged was equally brave and praiseworthy.

The concluding observations I have to make are brief, simply that immediately receiving the news and sending out directions to all stations on the division and Supt. Pearn 'J', which I afterwards found had already been done by officers at different times on their initiative, I drove to the scene with my groom and a P.C. in plain clothes armed with a revolver and ammunition, taking a direct course to Woodford, that being the last place where I heard the murderers were making for. When I reached the Napier arms P.H. Woodford, I was informed by Police scouts of the death of Jacob at the cottage nearby and the arrest of Helfeld.

I proceeded there and took general charge.

(sgd) W. Jenkins.
Superintendent.

Postscript

During the nineteenth, and the early part of the twentieth centuries, London had become a haven for numerous political revolutionaries, particularly from Russia. Karl Marx, Lenin, Trotsky, and it is believed even Stalin, had all at some time found sanctuary in the capital. Both the anarchists involved in the Tottenham incident were probably from Riga in the Baltic state of Latvia, which in 1905 had rebelled against the rule of the Tsar.

The gun used by Hefeld was a .32 Browning, and Jacob (Lepidus) carried a 6.5mm Bergmann. Between the two of them they fired over 400 rounds during the chase.

The man referred to as Helfeld in the report was Paul Hefeld (21), and known by the nickname 'Elephant'. After shooting himself, he lingered on for a few days before he succumbed to an infection and died.

Jacob was known to Special Branch as Jacob Lepidus or Meyer (25). He had worked at the rubber factory for a short while, and was obviously the source of information about the movement of the money.

Both men were buried in the same unmarked plot in the Queens Road Cemetery.

Awards

A new award for bravery, the King's Police Medal, was minted and the first was posthumously awarded to William Frederick Tyler, PC 403 'N'.

Others who received the award were John Cater, PC 714 'N'; Charles Dixon, Detective Constable CID; and Charles Eagles, PC 636 'N'.

Two constables were promoted to the rank of sergeant without taking the usual exam, and nine others were given cash awards for their part in the incident.

Other cash awards were made to several people involved in the chase, while there were many claims for compensation in respect of damage to property.

PC Tyler and the boy Ralph Joscelyne were buried in adjoining graves in Abney Park Cemetery.

II

HAWLEY HARVEY CRIPPEN

Those who knew or met him said that he was a very quietly spoken man who hated loud noises. He was studious and retiring by nature, and very cool in his attitude towards others. Born in Coldwater, Michigan, in 1862, he was not very tall, just 5 feet 3 inches, with a greying bushy moustache and wispy light-coloured hair. He had piercing grey eyes, which were magnified by the thick lenses of his gold-rimmed spectacles. When he walked his shoulders were hunched, and he threw his feet outwards as if trained as a dancer.

This was Dr Hawley Harvey Crippen, the man who was at the centre of one of the most publicised trials of the century, and who represented one of the saddest examples of a lover who killed for the sake of his relationship. As a case it is an interesting one, for whenever the circumstances are examined there is always an aspect of it which gives an extra insight into Crippen's background, and while not justifying his actions one begins to build up a certain empathy with his predicament.

Crippen's mistress Ethel Le Neve was twenty-seven years of age, a slightly built woman, just a little taller than her lover. She had known Crippen for nearly ten years before the events which led to their final separation overtook them, and for at least two or three of those years they had enjoyed an intimate personal relationship.

She worked as a shorthand typist in the same building where he was employed as the general manager of a company which sold all manner of patent medicines and remedies for minor illnesses.

His marriage was a failure, inasmuch as his wife Cora was an overbearing and dominant woman, whose ambitions to become a music-hall star were more important to her than marriage to this small, insignificant and passive man. More than once she had threatened to leave him, a threat which he shrugged off as just a display of her artistic temperament, but it was this continuing conflict of their personalities that was to lead to tragedy. It was on Monday 31 January 1910, at their rented Victorian four-storeyed house, at 39, Hilldrop Crescent, N.7, that matters came to a head. The Crippens were hosts at a dinner to some long-standing friends: a retired music-hall mime artiste, Paul Martinetti, and his wife Clara. Having dined and retired to the upstairs parlour to play whist, and indulge in the small talk that friends exchange at such homely meetings, Mr Martinetti expressed a wish to visit the bathroom. He was not feeling very well and Crippen assumed that he would know where to go, but he did not, and Cora berated him for not looking after the comfort of their guest. When the Martinettis left at 1.30am, as the front door closed Cora again started to scream and shout at her husband for his lack of attention to Mr Martinetti's needs, and once more repeated the threat she had made many times before, that she would leave him.

Little did Mrs Martinetti realise when she turned and waved good night, that it was to be the last time she would see her friend alive. What happened next is pure conjecture. It is probable that before she went to bed Cora partook of a glass of stout, to which she was partial, just to help her sleep. It is also probable that it was laced with a fatal dose of hyoscine hydrobromide, for Hawley Harvey Crippen had finally had enough of her rantings, ravings and threats.

At noon on the following day, Crippen called at the Martinetti flat in Shaftesbury Avenue, ostensibly to inquire about Paul's health, and found he had taken to his bed. When Clara inquired as to how Mrs Crippen was, he told her she was perfectly all right and in good spirits. But there is little doubt that when he made that visit, he had already murdered his wife and was well advanced in dissecting and disposing of the body.

Mrs Crippen had been an enthusiastic member of the Music Hall Ladies' Guild, and when they held their meeting on 2 February, in a room that Crippen allowed them to use at his place of business, Cora, who had been most assiduous in her duties as the honorary treasurer, was conspicuous by her absence. Soon after the meeting had started, Miss Ethel Le Neve, Crippen's secretary, entered and presented the guild's secretary, Miss May, with two letters of resignation. The letters were typed and signed with Mrs Crippen's stage name, Bella Elmore, and stated she had been obliged to return to America to deal with illness in her family. The members present were surprised, for there had been no indication of such a problem from the garrulous Cora.

They were even more surprised eighteen days later, when Crippen turned up at a dinner and ball organised by the guild, with Ethel Le Neve on his arm. It was noticed she was wearing some of Cora's jewellery and clothes. Inquiries as to his wife's wellbeing were met with glib answers and excuses, but these deceptions were soon to lead to Crippen's downfall. By March he had installed his mistress in the house at Hilldrop Crescent and had started to write letters to Cora's many friends, telling them she had gone away. Later he concocted a series of letters telling them a story of how she had died while in America. There was little that could be described as subtle about Crippen. With every attempt to cover his tracks he compounded his guilt. On 15 March he wrote a letter to his landlord, giving three months' notice of his intention to leave, and on the morning of 24 March a telegram from Victoria Station arrived at the Martinettis' house informing them of Cora's demise, and Crippen's intention of going away for a while to get over the shock. Two days later an obituary notice appeared, in *The Era,* a show-business paper, telling the readers that Bella Elmore was dead. To make the story more convincing, he had memorial cards printed.

Crippen was telling the truth when he said he was going away. On the evening of 23 March, the two lovers caught the boat train to spend Easter in Dieppe. When he boarded the boat he was carrying a heavy bag. When he disembarked at Dieppe, he no longer had the bag with him. It was generally believed that he threw it overboard, and what it contained was probably the last piece of the body that he was keen to dispose of – Cora's head.

April and May passed, and Crippen's confidence grew. He informed the landlord that he would now be staying at Hilldrop Crescent for a little while longer, but then there occurred an unexpected problem. Answering a knock at the front door, Crippen found some old friends of Cora's, Mr and Mrs Nash, standing on his doorstep. They had recently returned from a tour of the halls in America and had called to renew their acquaintance with their old friend Cora. When they heard the sad news of her death, they became curious, and questioned Crippen at some length about the circumstances of her demise. When they left they were not satisfied with his answers and went to visit another old friend, Detective Superintendent Froest, the man in charge of Scotland Yard's Murder Squad. He too was curious when they told him about the disappearance of Mrs Crippen, and he quickly assigned an officer to make inquiries about the circumstances of her absence.

On Friday 8 July in the late morning, Detective Chief Inspector Dew, with Detective Sergeant Mitchell, climbed the stairs that led to the front door of 39, Hilldrop Crescent. The door was opened by a French maid, who having inquired as to the purpose of their visit, ushered them into the hallway, where they were met by Miss Le Neve. They noticed she was wearing a brooch, the same brooch that had been described to them by members of the theatre guild who they had interviewed during their preliminary inquiries.

When she heard who they were, she blanched a little, and then disappeared upstairs. There was a mumbled conversation, and Dew watched as a man with a heavy moustache slowly descended the stairs. Dew introduced himself.

'I am Detective Chief Inspector Dew, and this is Detective Sergeant Mitchell. Some of your wife's friends have been to us concerning the stories you have told them about her death, with which they are not satisfied. I have made exhaustive inquiries, and I am not satisfied, so I have come to see you to ask if you care to offer an explanation.'

Crippen reacted to this precise introduction with an air of resignation, and conducted them upstairs to the parlour where after a discussion, he agreed to dictate a statement. Mitchell laboriously wrote it down. He gave an account of the background to his life, and explained the circumstances of how his first wife died. How he had met and married Cora Turner, and then discovered that her name was not Cora Turner, but Kunigunde Mackamotski, who had been born in a Brooklyn slum. He related how he had spent a lot of money training her to fulfil her aspirations to pursue a career on the stage as a singer. When he objected to her desire to sing on the music halls, he explained how her attitude towards him had changed. They had stopped sleeping together, and occupied separate rooms in the house. While he had been away on a business trip to America, he heard she had been singing at smoking concerts, and seeing a man called Bruce Miller. He inferred that she might have eloped with the latter and justified his reasons for announcing to everyone that she was dead by saying that he did not want to be subjected to the embarrassment of telling everyone that she had left him for someone else. There were few alternative reasons that he could offer to her friends about her disappearance.

He explained how Miller, a music-hall artiste, used to visit his wife and give her money to buy presents. He knew because he had read love letters that had been written to her. He spoke of her threats to leave him, and how she had made it plain that Miller could support her in a better lifestyle than the one which Crippen offered her. He expanded his explanation, telling the detectives that he thought Cora had gone to Chicago with Miller, to advance her career as a music-hall singer. As he dictated his deposition he created a web of half-truths, those statements which have both the elements of truth and the lie, and which for the detective are the most difficult to prove or disprove. When he had finished his statement, he showed the detectives around the house, and produced the letters Miller had written. He said he realised how silly he had been inventing the story of Cora's death, but how could he help to clear the matter up? Together with Dew, Crippen composed an advertisement which he promised to circulate in American newspapers, agreeing to pay a reward if she was found. He knew there was little chance of that.

At 8pm, after an exhausting day Dew and Mitchell left the house, but they were not convinced. Their minds were outlining another scenario about the disappearance of Mrs Crippen, and they were more determined than ever to satisfy their intuition.

First, a missing person's description was circulated to every police station in London, and Dew and Mitchell worked over the weekend checking on what Crippen had told them. On Monday morning they went to interview their suspect again, but he was not at home nor was he at his office. The little moustached lover had flown with his mistress.

Dew immediately widened his search, circulating their description to all ports. Now, having obtained a warrant, he began a detailed search of the house. First he looked in the garden, examining the ground for evidence of a burial, and then he began an inspection of the house – in particular, the coal cellar. Initially he found nothing, but not satisfied, he returned and looked again the following day, again with no result. On Thursday he was still searching around the house and garden, but his instinct led him back to the cellar. He stared hard at the brick floor, and went down on his hands and knees to examine it in more detail. He returned upstairs to the kitchen where he found a poker, and returning to the cellar he started to probe the floor. He found that the end of the poker could easily be pushed between two of the bricks, and as he prised upwards, first one brick came away, and then another, and another. He got a spade and started to dig at the underlying clay. He dug deeper, and deeper, then he stopped, stood up, and stepped back from his excavation. Staring at the hole for a few moments, he spoke tersely.

'Go and get the Divisional Surgeon.'

He had found what was left of Cora Crippen.

It was early evening when Dew and Dr Marshall began inspecting the opening in the middle of the floor. More digging was necessary to expose the entire remains, and the following day Dr Pepper, a pathologist, began to examine the contents in more detail. The soil was mixed with lime, and they found some partially bleached dark brown hair, twisted round a Hinde curler. There was a knotted decaying handkerchief, some pieces of cloth, and part of a woman's undervest. More importantly there was a man's pyjama jacket with a label on it.

They found pieces of skin, fat, and muscle tissue from the thigh and the buttocks. Most of the body organs were there: the heart, liver, kidneys and spleen. What they did not find were the bones. Whoever had buried the body had managed to remove the entire skeletal frame, along with those human parts which could positively identify the sex of the victim. This was not the work of an amateur. It was that of a professional, someone with a good knowledge of anatomy, a doctor perhaps.

Dew and Mitchell began the long task of preparing the

evidence for a murder trial. But first they had to find the whereabouts of Doctor Hawley Harvey Crippen and his mistress, Ethel Le Neve.

Whether Le Neve knew how Crippen had killed and disposed of his wife is uncertain, but her instinct told her they would have to get away from England if they were to enjoy their lives together. After Dew's visit, they had gathered what belongings they could, and caught a boat train to Brussels. After spending a few days there, they went on to Rotterdam and then to Antwerp. On 20 July the SS *Montrose*, a 5,431-ton cargo vessel which had been converted to carry passengers to the New World, pointed her bows towards the sea and steamed down the River Scheldt, bound for Canada, with a river pilot at the helm. Her Captain, Henry Kendall, temporarily relieved of the immediate responsibility of command, went to his cabin. Glancing through a window he saw two of his second-class passengers standing at the rail watching the river bank slipping by. One was a short clean-shaven man, dressed in a brown suit, white canvas shoes and a grey brimmed hat on his head. Standing next to him was a gangly youth whose trousers seemed too small for him, for they had split at the back and held together by a large safety pin. Kendall's curiosity was aroused even more when he noticed they were holding and squeezing each other's hands. He was quoted later in a newspaper report as saying, 'It seemed to me unnatural for two males, so I suspected them at once.'

A check of his passenger list showed that they were Mr John Philo Robinson and his sixteen-year-old son, also called John, who, when he did say anything, which was seldom, spoke with a high-pitched feminine voice. Robinson on the other hand went to great lengths to tell everyone in his cultured American accent, that he was taking his son Master Robinson to a warmer climate for his health, and that he intended to make for California which he felt would suit his boy's condition.

Captain Kendall had read about the search for Crippen

and his lover, and was determined to satisfy his feelings about the true identity of these two passengers. He asked his officers to quietly remove any copies of current newspapers which they found lying around, to avoid the chance of the suspects becoming aware of the publicity that their case had attracted. Without arousing their suspicions he checked their descriptions with the authorities in England, using his new Marconi wireless telegraph system. Crippen, for his part, enjoying the relaxation of a boat trip, sat in a deck chair and read *The Four Just Men*, a book about a fictional murder in London, unaware of his exposure in the papers or the inquiries that were being made. Ethel, dressed in her boy's costume, played

> The first person to be caught by a telegraph message was John Tawell, a Quaker, who on New Year's Day 1845 poisoned Sarah Hart at her house in Salt Hill, Slough. Someone became suspicious of him when he was boarding a train for Paddington and a message was sent up the line on the newly installed telegraph system. When Tawell arrived at the terminus, he was followed to his lodging house by a railway official, where he was later arrested.

with any young children who happened to be on deck. If they had looked up, they might have wondered why there was so much electrical crackling coming from the wires strung between the ship's masts.

It was on 22 July that Walter Dew saw the cables from Captain Kendall. He wasted no time in making arrangements for himself and Sergeant Mitchell to obtain passage on the SS *Laurentic*. This was a much faster ship and would arrive in Quebec days before the *Montrose*. On 23 July they set sail out of Liverpool for Canada.

Father Point is a headland near the entrance of the St Lawrence river. From here ships pick up their pilots, to guide them through the hazards of the river, to a safe harbour in

Quebec. Crippen watched as the pilot boat approached the side of the *Montrose*, and he must have been thinking that his freedom was likely to be short-lived. He later said that he had been told by one of the ship's quartermasters that he would be arrested when the ship docked in Montreal. He told a story of entering into an agreement with this man, whereby for a sum of money he would be hidden on board, and it would be reported that he had fallen over the side. He had even prepared suicide notes to impress the idea that he had committed suicide.

Crippen watched as the pilot boat drew alongside and two men dressed in dark blue reefer jackets, with caps pulled over their eyes, climbed the ladder thrown over the side. What he did not know or expect was that they were Dew and Mitchell, and to say that he was surprised when they appeared at his cabin door is to put it mildly. 'Good morning Dr Crippen. I am Inspector Dew. I am here to arrest you for the murder and mutilation of your wife, Cora Crippen, in London on or about 2 February last.' The words left Crippen drained of all response. He sagged down on the bunk and stared vacantly at the floor.

Extradition proceedings began in Quebec on 8 August; twelve days later , the SS *Megantic* steamed out of Montreal, bound for Liverpool. As she sailed downriver, a tug pulled alongside and a ladder was lowered from a loading door in the ship's side. Five people clambered up into the safety of the hull. They were Ethel Le Neve, handcuffed to a wardress; Dr Hawley Harvey Crippen, handcuffed to Sergeant Mitchell; and Chief Inspector Walter Dew. The latter had not only caught his suspects, but had succeeded in avoiding the curiosity of the world press. During the few days' respite before the ship docked in Liverpool, the two lovers met only once. Crippen asked to see Le Neve, and they were brought to their respective cabin doors. No words passed between them: only their eyes spoke. Having stared at each other for a few moments, Crippen averted his gaze, turned away, and went back into his cabin. They would not meet again until they stood in the dock at Bow Street.

Their arrival at Liverpool on 28 August was a noisy affair. They were greeted by crowds of shouting and screaming people, both at Liverpool and when they arrived later at Euston Station. They were taken straight to Scotland Yard and Crippen was housed in a cell in Cannon Row police station. Later he was transferred to Bow Street where committal proceedings opened on the 29th. Three days later both Crippen and Le Neve were committed for trial at the Old Bailey. Today the cell that Crippen was kept in at Cannon Row police station no longer houses those who have been arrested. It has been converted into an office used by policemen responsible for the security of the Houses of Parliament.

The Trial

It was Tuesday 18 October 1910 when the trial opened in front of the Lord Chief Justice of England, the Right Honourable Lord Alverstone. The counsel for the crown were Mr R. D. Muir, assisted by Mr Travers Humphreys, and Mr Ingleby Oddie; Crippen was represented by Mr Tobin KC, assisted by Mr Huntley Jenkins and Mr Roome.

The Clerk of the court intoned the charge. 'Hawley Harvey Crippen, you are indicted and also charged on the coroner's inquisition with the wilful murder of Cora Crippen on 1 February last. Are you guilty or not guilty?'.

Crippens voice was clear and positive.

'Not guilty, my Lord.'

The stage was set for some dramatic revelations during the next five days.

The First Day
Muir opened for the prosecution with an outline of the case, and then pursued his brief by presenting a series of witnesses as to facts and events.

Two of the most important were examined on the first day. Mrs Clara Martinetti told of when she had last seen Cora, the visit to her flat by Crippen, and the jewellery she had seen Ethel Le Neve wearing at the ball. When questioned she also described a scar she had seen on the lower part of Cora's stomach, and the colour of her hair.

Bruce Miller travelled all the way over from America, a long boat trip in those days, to answer only one relevant question for the prosecution. After describing his background, Mr Muir asked him whether Bella Elmore had gone to live with him in America as Crippen had claimed. His reply was short and sharp.

'I never heard of such a thing.'

In cross-examination Tobin for the defence tried to educe evidence of an illicit relationship, to detract from Miller's reliability as a witness, but apart from the production of some letters written by him to her and evidence of them meeting, there was little Tobin could do to undermine Miller's initial reply to Muir's question, which helped to disprove what Crippen had said in his original statement.

More supportive evidence was given by a series of witnesses to prove letters written by Crippen, and identification of Cora's jewellery. Ethel Le Neve's landlady told of how her tenant had been given a lot of Cora's clothes. Evidence of Crippen's occupancy of the house at Hilldrop Crescent and of his financial affairs ended the first day's hearing, and the court adjourned.

The Second Day

Chief Inspector Dew took the stand at the beginning of the second day. Having introduced himself to the court, he produced the statement dictated to him by Crippen at Hilldrop Crescent. Mr Travers Humphreys slowly read out the statement to the hushed court, stressing those parts which he intended to disprove. Dew outlined what he had found in the house, telling the court about the three pairs of pyjamas, one of which had the jacket missing. Then he related the steps taken to find the former occupants of 39, Hilldrop Crescent, finishing with their arrest on the *Montrose*. The cross-examination of Dew by the defence failed to produce any facts which could undermine his evidence.

Slowly the prosecution built up the case against Crippen, based on the statement he had made.

Pathological evidence given by Dr Augustus Joseph Pepper told the story of the grisly remains buried in the basement.

What exactly had been found?

Were they the remains of a man or woman?

How long in his opinion had the remains been buried?

What exactly was the mark he had found when examining a piece of skin from the lower part of the front portion of the abdomen?

Slowly Muir drew from his expert witness fact after fact, which with methodical logic discredited Crippen's alleged innocence. The court listened in silent awe as Pepper described how he had been unable to find any bones or organs of generation, which could definitely identify whether the remains found in the grave were male or female. There was only a piece of decomposed flesh with what appeared to be the impression of an old operational scar. 'It was the mark of a scar, a little over four inches in length. When that piece was in position on the human body, in my opinion it was in the middle line in front, it may have been a little to the left; it began just above the pubes and extended for four inches or a little over. The whole scar was complete. There was a piece of flesh beyond it. It was quite an old scar. There was no trace of any genitals at all, or any certain anatomical indication of sex. There was hair on that piece of flesh, in my opinion pubic hair.'

Pepper followed with evidence of a piece of pyjama jacket that he had found in the grave. The collar was still attached and on it there was a label with the wording 'Shirtmakers, Jones Brothers, Holloway Ltd, Holloway, N.' The material was similar to that of two other pairs of pyjamas found in the house. They bore exactly the same label.

More evidence followed, about the expertise of the person

who had removed and placed the viscera in the cellar grave, leading to the opinion that the operation had been carried out with a great degree of skill, by someone with a good degree of experience.

Pepper related how he had examined a Hinde curler with a tuft of hair in it, which was shaded from dark to light brown. He had compared this with hair seen at the mortuary, and he was of the opinion that they were the same colour and from the same woman. Cross-examination by Tobin attempted to discredit Pepper's evidence of how and why he came to his views on the pieces of hair, flesh, and viscera. Arguments as to whether the marks on the skin were in fact scar tissue, or whether they had been caused by pressure of the material in which they were wrapped, failed to shake Pepper's evidence in chief.

Finally he stated that, in his opinion, the remains had been buried for no longer than eight months.

As he stepped down from the box, the court broke into a chatter of muted conversation. The court usher shouted 'Silence in court', and the judge pronounced that the case would be adjourned until the following day.

The Third Day

The first witness into the box on the third day was Dr Bernard Henry Spilsbury from St Mary's Hospital. He had been recognised as having the potential of being a good pathologist at an early stage in his career, and had spent many years learning his profession both medically and legally in numerous mortuaries and coroners' courts. This was to be the first big criminal case that he was to appear in.

Humphreys questioned him about a sample of flesh that had been given to him for examination. His explanation was short and to the point. It was, in his opinion, a piece of flesh from the lower part of the abdominal wall, near the middle. His conclusion was arrived at after examination under the microscope, and the identification of glands on either side. It was, without doubt, an old operational scar. A request by the jury to see the pieces in question resulted in them being passed around the court on a soup plate.

Humphreys sat down and Tobin rose to his feet. His questions, phrased to raise an element of doubt in the minds of the jurors, failed to shake the evidence of the young pathologist. Humphreys' re-examination endorsed the fact that the pieces were from the body of Mrs Crippen.

More witnesses followed and then Dr Willcox was called. Having identified a number of exhibits he began to explain in detail what he had found in his forensic examination of the viscera. He told the court of how he had carried out tests and found mydriatic vegetable alkaloid, of which there are three types (atropine, hyoscyamin and hyoscine) in the samples. The one present in the samples was hyoscine. It was normally a drug that was injected in small quantities, but could be administered orally if disguised, by giving it in sweet tea, coffee, or even stout.

Cross-examination by the defence failed to shake the doctor's professional opinion that the drug was hyoscine. Although he was aware before making his analysis that Crippen had purchased five grains of the drug, it did not alter the truth of the facts relating to what he had found.

Willcox's evidence was supported by Dr Luff, the next witness called, and then Mr Charles Hetherington, a chemist employed at Lewis and Burrows of 108, New Oxford Street, who told how Crippen had ordered and later purchased five grains of the drug hyoscine hydrobromide earlier in the year, either on 17 or 18 January. More witnesses supported the credibility of evidence already given, and Muir sat down well satisfied with the way he had presented the case for the Crown.

What he had shown was that Crippen's statement was a lie. He had purchased poison, killed his wife with it, and then cut up and disposed of her body by burying it in the basement of 39, Hilldrop Crescent. He had then attempted to avoid arrest by changing his identity, and going to America. It was all pretty damning evidence.

★

Tobin opened the defence with a speech to the court outlining his client's situation, trying to give the impression that he was a much maligned man who was innocent of the accusations made against him.

He called his first witness. It was Crippen himself. Mr Huntley Jenkins took him through the story of his life. Crippen spoke of his training, his marriage, his movements, and was quick to stress that he had not had the sort of pathological training that would have enabled him to cut up and de-bone Mrs Crippen. He made play of her association with Bruce Miller, her vain attempts to prolong the relationship being the reason for her disappearance. He spoke about his need for drugs in his work as a homoeopathic doctor, and in particular hyoscine. He needed little prompting from his counsel, and apart from the odd interjection by the Lord Chief Justice to clear up a point in the evidence, he gave an articulate account of his story to the court. When he had finished the court adjourned.

The evidence in chief had been given, and now Muir's cross-examination would have to wait until the following day Friday 21 October 1910.

The Fourth Day
The queues for the public gallery stretched along the street. Far more people wanted to listen to the day's hearing than it was possible to accommodate. Only the few who had written and been granted a seat out of the thousands of applications would be able to witness the events. By the time the court sat, the gallery was crammed to capacity.

Muir started his cross-examination. He wasted little time in coming to the point, commencing with questions to Crippen about his wife.

When had he last seen her?

Had he prepared breakfast for her on the fateful day when she had allegedly walked out of the house alive?

Had he made any inquiries concerning her whereabouts?

What had she taken with her?

How much money did he give her?

How much money had he got from pawning her jewellery?

What had he done with it?

Relentlessly Muir put his questions to the bespectacled man in the dock, interrupted only by the Lord Chief Justice clarifying a point for the benefit of the jury. They continued.

When had Ethel Le Neve come to live at Hilldrop Crescent? There were questions concerning the telegram he had sent to the Martinettis, and the letters he had written telling of Bella's death. His trip to Dieppe with Ethel. The letters were read out to the hushed court, everyone listening intently to the drama being enacted in front of them in this theatre of real life.

Muir now stopped sparring, and began to jab at Crippen verbally with his comments.

'Do you ask the jury to believe . . .?'

'You are telling lies which you hope will be believed.'

Crippen's credibility was being articulately exposed to the court. More questions followed getting him to elaborate on his statements and actions. Muir asked about his association with Ethel Le Neve, then he changed his line of inquiry to questions about the cellar and the use of coal in the house. It all appeared very innocent, until he asked about the remains in the cellar and started a line of questioning about pyjamas.

'Now I want you to look please at the two suits of pyjamas.'

Crippen was handed the two sets.

'Are those your pyjamas?'

'They are.'

'When did you get them?'

'I think I bought them last September.'

'You mean September 1909?'

'Yes.'

'Did you buy them yourself?'

'Yes, I bought them myself.' There was a note of agitation in Crippen's voice, but Muir continued with his precise, icily polite, questioning.

'Where?'

'At Jones Brothers.'

'Had you any other suits of pyjamas at the time?' Muir's voice was quizzical.

'There were my worn-out ones.'

Question followed question on the mundane subject of pyjamas as Muir slowly drew Crippen into a trap.

His replies about the garments were not convincing. Muir did not hurry him, giving Crippen every chance to change his answers if he wished. Muir produced a pair of pyjama trousers and asked the accused when he had purchased them. He admitted to 1905.

'Were they purchased along with the other two pairs?'

'No they were old ones, part of another purchase.'

Muir, with a relentless flow of logical questioning, proved that the three sets of pyjamas found in the house, one pair of which had the jacket missing, had all been purchased in 1909 and were all made from the same batch of material. Crippen tried to confuse the issue, but his answers were not convincing. He became confused and lost in the labyrinth of lies he had tried to create.

Muir delved into his reasons for fleeing the country and the elaborate disguises adopted by himself and Le Neve to avoid recognition. He was taken carefully through the sequence of events which led to his arrest, and in particular his reasons for arranging a mock suicide, allegedly involving one of the ship's quartermasters. Muir read out the suicide note that Crippen had written on the back of a visiting card printed in the name of Robinson, and that Crippen had intended leaving in his cabin.

'I cannot stand the horrors I go through every night any longer, and as I see nothing bright ahead and money has come to an end, I have made up my mind to jump overboard to-night. I know I have spoilt your life, but hope some day you can learn to forgive me; with last words of love. Your H.'

By now the speed of Muir's questions had increased. No longer slow and methodical, they were fired in short sharp bursts. Crippen, weary after hours in the witness box, gave more and more unconvincing replies to the questions put to him. It was not over for him. When Muir sat down, having finished his examination, he was re-examined by his own counsel, in an attempt to bring back some credibility to his story. When he left the box, he must have realised that it was all over for him.

The defence medical witnesses did little to help his cause. Dr Turnbull, a Director of the Pathological Institute, could not make up his mind as to a positive identification of the piece of flesh that he had been called on to examine, at one stage even stating to the court that he had not wanted to give evidence. Other doctors called were no more convincing.

There was one last riposte by Muir to destroy the defence case. He called an extra witness for the prosecution: a Mr Chilvers who was an employee of Jones Brothers. He stated that he had a record of sending the pyjamas to 39, Hilldrop Crescent, the bill to be paid cash on delivery. When asked to state whether the jacket found in the grave matched the trousers found in the house, he replied, 'Yes. I have seen the tab on the part which is in the jar and it bears the words Jones Brothers, Holloway Limited. Jones Brothers have been a limited company since 1906.'

This simple reply proved quite conclusively that Crippen had lied when he told the court he had purchased the pyjamas in 1905. At that time the company was not a limited one.

All that now remained were the closing speeches of the counsel and the summing-up by the judge.

The Fifth Day

It was 2.15pm on Saturday 22 October when the jury retired to consider their verdict. They returned to the court 37 minutes later. There was a buzz of excitement as the judge in his red gown returned to his seat. The jury slowly filed back and resumed their places, then the clerk rose from his seat in the well of the court and facing the jury box addressed the foreman. 'Gentleman have you agreed upon your verdict?' 'We have'. 'Do you find the prisoner guilty or not guilty of wilful murder?' Everyone had their eyes fixed intently on the Foreman of the Jury. 'We find the prisoner guilty of wilful murder.'

Crippen stared at the judge through his thick lenses, and leaning on the front rail of the dock bent forward and said weakly, 'I still protest my innocence.'

Lord Alverstone placed the black cap on his head, and intoned the sentence of death.

The case was over. The counsel picked up their papers. The public gallery emptied. By 3pm the only people in the court were the cleaners, going about their sweeping and polishing.

The following week on Tuesday 25 October, Ethel Le Neve was tried for being an accessory after the fact in the murder of Cora Crippen. She was represented by Frederick Edwin Smith who was, at the time, the youngest King's Counsel in the country. The judge was again Lord Alverstone and the Crown was represented by the same advocates that had obtained the conviction of Crippen.

The prosecution case was an abbreviated form of the evidence given in Crippen's trial. When the prosecuting counsel had finished, Mr F. E. Smith for the defence announced his intention of not calling any evidence for the defence. It was a clever move on Smith's part, for it was obvious that in his speech for the defence he was going to make an emotional plea to the jury.

Tobin's closing speech was short and to the point without any embellishments. Smith followed with his impassioned address to the jury. What they had to decide was whether Le Neve had assisted her lover in killing his wife. It was left to the Lord Chief Justice to give a sympathetic summing-up.

It was twelve minutes past four when the jury filed back into the court. The verdict 'Not guilty.' In less than a day, Ethel Le Neve had been acquitted.

All that was left was an appeal by Crippen, which was

dismissed. However, he made one last attempt to escape the scaffold. He planned to puncture an artery with the arm of his spectacles, but his intention was discovered before he could carry it out.

On the morning of Wednesday 23 November, Hawley Harvey Crippen met the executioner John Ellis in the condemned cell at Pentonville prison. With his hands and feet tied he stood on the trap door, the hood over his head. At the first stroke of eight o'clock, Ellis pushed the lever forward and Crippen dropped into oblivion.

The first use of wireless telegraph

Dr Hawley Harvey Crippen, and his mistress Ethel Le Neve, who were wanted for the murder of Mrs Cora Crippen in 1910, were the first persons to be caught by the use of wireless telegraph. They had boarded the SS *Montrose* at Antwerp and were on their way to Canada. The alert Captain Kendall spotted them and when the ship was two days out, sent a message back to England alerting the authorities. Inspector Dew, in charge of the case, caught a faster boat and intercepted the *Montrose* before she docked in Quebec, arresting the suspects.

Wireless telegraph in those days was operated by means of transmitting from one boat to another, a method necessary to combat the curvature of the earth.

What happened to Ethel

After Crippen was hanged, Le Neve changed her name to Harvey. In 1914 she met a man called Smith who was a sergeant in the army. They subsequently married and had two children, a boy and a girl. They lived near Bournemouth where Ethel ran a teashop. She died around 1969. When I met her son years later neither he nor his sister had any idea of their mother's identity. She never discussed the case, and she would very seldom agree to having her picture taken.

12

GEORGE JOSEPH SMITH
THE WELSHER

Until the outbreak of the First World War, the early years of this century were a period when the population were absorbing themselves into a society of changing values. The railway had become an accepted part of life, and with it came the opportunity to travel quickly to places that people had previously only heard or read about. During the summer they would flock to the seaside and pleasure resorts, where they could enjoy the freedom and the different surroundings. Inevitably, there were, mixing with these crowds, opportunists who saw a way of making easy money: thieves, pickpockets, and confidence tricksters who relieved the visitors of their hard-earned cash.

There were others whose reasons for visiting the seaside resorts had a much more sinister purpose. Such a man was George Joseph Smith.

Smith had been involved in crime all his life. Born in 1872 in the East End of London, he was sent to a reformatory at the age of nine where he remained until he was sixteen. Already a hardened criminal he spent his teens in and out of prison for such offences as burglary, receiving stolen property, and obtaining money by false pretences. It was a pattern of criminal behaviour that Smith followed during the whole of his miserable life.

In 1897 and recently released from prison, he found work as a baker in Leicester, where he met and married an eighteen-year-old shopgirl, Caroline Thornhill. Smith saw her as a meal ticket, for he had little intention of doing any honest work himself when his wife could be sent out to earn money. After their wedding, he left his job and they travelled to the south coast; there Caroline obtained employment as a domestic. Smith was a man with a dominant and forceful personality, and he bullied and threatened his wife into stealing whatever she could from her employers. Soon both their names appeared in police 'Wanted' notices, and they were obliged to move continually from one seaside town to another until eventually Caroline was arrested in Eastbourne on a charge of being in possession of stolen goods. Smith did not wait to ascertain the results of her trial. Hearing she was in custody, he immediately caught a train to London where he found lodgings near Victoria. He now began to use a method he was to employ time and time again. As he was short of funds, and wanted free bed and board, he convinced his elderly landlady that he had fallen in love with her, and made a proposal of marriage. She, flattered by his attentions, agreed and they went through the formalities of his first bigamous marriage. He could now once again sit back and enjoy life, without the worry of working for a living. As with Caroline, his new 'wife' was paying for everything.

Meanwhile Caroline had served her one-year prison sentence, and when released returned to London and found work. By chance she was walking down Oxford Street in late November 1900, when she saw Smith looking in a shop window. Embittered by the callous way he had treated her, she called a policeman to arrest him. Smith, taken completely by surprise, became abusive and threatening, but she was adamant that he would suffer as she had. Charges of receiving were laid against him, for which he received a sentence of two years' hard labour. She, frightened of what he might do to her when he was released, emigrated to Canada.

On his release, Smith returned to his bigamous wife, who told him she had no intention of supporting him while he did nothing. Realising that he could no longer sponge on her for money, he responded with a fit of violent rage and viciously attacked her. Having gratified his temper, he took what money he could find, and what articles he could pawn, and walked out.

By 1908 Smith was living in Bristol and calling himself an antiques dealer. He had made another conquest and entered into a further 'marriage' with a woman named Edith Peglar. It appears that he had a genuine affection for this woman, for although he left her a number of times to contract other bigamous marriages, he always returned to her.

A year later we find him in Southampton persuading yet another gullible lady to marry him. Posing as Mr Rose, an antiques dealer, he rushed Miss Sarah Freeman to the local Register Office to tie the knot. Formalities completed, they left to find accommodation in Clapham and within three days he had managed to inveigle all her money out of her. With his pockets lined with her cash, he decided that it would be good for Sarah to have an interesting day out at the National Gallery. While looking around, he made an excuse that he wanted to relieve himself, and left her looking at the paintings. When he failed to return, Sarah went home, only to find the he had cleared the flat of all her clothes and possessions, including her nest-egg of some £350, leaving her penniless.

With Sarah's money Smith went to Southend where he purchased a house, contacted the faithful Miss Peglar and asked her to join him. They stayed in the seaside town for a while and then returned to Bristol, where in August 1910 he met Bessie Mundy. The latter was bowled over by his amorous attentions, and within days of their meeting he had whisked her off to Weymouth where he followed his usual *modus operandi*, going through a marriage ceremony at the local Register Office. Although Mundy had quite a considerable sum of money, it was paid as a monthly income and Smith was unable to get his hands on it. After some weeks he tired of the effort to wheedle it out of her, accused her of giving him venereal disease, and disappeared to go back and live with Edith.

Two years later, in March 1912, Bessie Mundy was walking along the windswept seafront at Weston-super-Mare, when she saw Smith strolling along the promenade towards her. It is difficult to determine who was the more surprised, but Smith realised that this chance encounter gave him another opportunity to get hold of her money, and he suggested a reconciliation. It was now that Bessie Mundy made her fatal mistake – she agreed to his suggestion.

Smith gave plenty of thought to how to acquire Mundy's money; he finally decided that the only way was by inheriting it on her death. He now began to plan with this in mind, first convincing her that they should both make wills where in the event of death each would inherit the other's estate. She agreed, and having visited the solicitor's and made it legal and binding, they went to live at Herne Bay where they rented a small house which had no bathroom. Shortly after they had settled in, Smith took his wife to visit their local general practitioner, Dr French. She complained of having suffered a fit, which had resulted in her becoming unconscious. The doctor examined her but could find nothing wrong; however, he prescribed some medication. Other visits to his surgery followed with Mundy complaining of feeling ill, and there is good reason to believe that Smith was adding some form of toxic agent to her food, which was creating the condition.

In early July Smith purchased a tin bath from a local ironmonger. Unable to afford the full cost he agreed to leave a deposit of five shillings and promised to pay the rest later. On the morning of Saturday the 13th, Dr French was getting dressed before breakfast when he was handed a note with a cryptic message: 'Come at once. My wife is dead.' He hurried round to the house where Smith directed him to a room upstairs. As the doctor entered, he saw a tin bath filled with lukewarm water. Lying in it on her back, with her head completely submerged, was Bessie Mundy. She was dead.

The inquest revealed no evidence of foul play, and a verdict of accidental death was arrived at. Smith made rapid arrangements for Bessie to be buried in a pauper's grave, settled her affairs, and departed with the money and effects left to him in her will. Before going back to Bristol, he cleaned the bath and returned it to the ironmonger, saying that it was not suitable for his needs and requesting the return of his five shillings.

> The earliest recorded murder was in Sumer about 1850 BC, when three men were sentenced to death for killing a manservant called Inanna. It was recorded in Sumerian writings.

For over a year Smith lived off the £2,500 he had accrued from Bessie Mundy's death. It was a considerable sum at a time when the average wage was £2–£3 a week. However, he could not contain his greed, and once more he left Edith and went on his rounds of the seaside resorts in search of another victim. He found her in Southsea in October 1913, in the form of an ample twenty-five-year-old nurse named Alice Burnham. With what must have been an overwhelming charm, he persuaded her to 'marry' him. They were joined in not so holy matrimony on 4 November, and he took her off to live in Blackpool, where they rented a bedsitter with use of bathroom.

By now Smith had found a way of getting even more money from the death of his victims. Not satisfied with Alice's bank accounts, he took out an insurance on her life. Soon the new 'Mrs Smith' began to complain of headaches and a general malaise. She consulted a doctor but he could find nothing radically wrong and prescribed a mild sedative.

To achieve his ends, Smith now enacted an elaborate charade. On the evening of 12 December, he asked their landlady, Mrs Crossley, to prepare some hot water so that his wife could take a bath when they came back from a walk. Later that evening Mrs Crossley was sitting in her kitchen with her family, when they saw water coming through the ceiling and trickling down the walls. As she opened the kitchen door to investigate, Smith was standing there. In his hands he held two eggs which he said he would like for breakfast, and when she drew his attention to the water he rushed upstairs. He appeared a moment later, shouting for her to go and get a doctor. When Doctor Billing arrived he found Alice Burnham sitting in the bath with Smith supporting her head, her body covered with warm soapy water. She was quite dead.

An inquest followed, with Smith acquitting himself well with a fine piece of dramatic acting. His description of the events leading to the finding of the body were suitably peppered with breaks in his composure and floods of real tears. It certainly invoked the sympathy of the court and a verdict of accidental death was brought in. However, his histrionics and callous indifference to her death did not impress Mr and Mrs Crossley, who had hosted his contrived tragedy. The verdict was followed by the funeral service, arranged with indecent haste, and another pauper's grave.

Smith must have felt quite confident about his skills as a murderer when he travelled back to Peglar for Christmas with some £600 in his pocket. His next venture took place a month after war had been declared in September 1914. This time he went to Bournemouth where he found Miss Alice Reavil, a suitable subject upon which to practise his charm. Before the month was out, he had whisked her away to Woolwich and placed a brass ring on her finger. Again he got up to his old tricks. He took Alice for a tram ride to Battersea Park where he made an excuse to leave her. While she looked at the flowers and listened to the band, Smith made his way back to their rooms at Battersea Rise and cleaned out the house of all her belongings plus £90, whereupon he set out for Bristol and dear old Edith.

Smith's last visit to sign the marriage register was on 17 December 1914, and he chose of all places the city of Bath. He had met a rejected thirty-eight-year-old spinster Miss Margaret Lofty earlier in the year, and with his silken oratory persuaded her to marry him without her telling any of her relatives. He then followed the same procedures as before. First he convinced her to make a will leaving everything to him, and then took out an insurance policy payable to himself in the event of her sudden death, although she was in fact already insured.

On this occasion he wasted little time. Married on the Thursday, they went straight to the rooms he had found in Bismarck Road, Highgate. That night he took his 'wife' to the local doctor, where she complained of a headache. On Friday morning they attended at a solicitor's for the purpose of making their wills. On Friday afternoon he asked the landlady to prepare the water for a bath. At about eight o'clock in the evening she was ironing in the kitchen when she heard the splashing of water, followed shortly afterwards by the dulcet tones of the harmonium in her front room playing 'Nearer my God to Thee'. A few moments later she heard the front door slam. Shortly after, there was a loud knock at the front door. When she answered, Smith was standing there with a brown paper bag in his hand, making excuses for forgetting to use his key. He inquired whether his wife had come downstairs, saying he had just been out to buy some tomatoes for her breakfast.

There followed the usual processes of inquiry. The doctor was called and found nothing suspicious about the death. The police were informed. The coroner's officer took particulars. Funeral arrangements were made, and after thirty-eight naive years of life, Margaret Lofty was committed to the earth, her husband having managed to beat down the undertaker on the cost of the funeral. Because it was close to

Christmas the inquest was postponed until the early part of the New Year. Smith, satisfied that he had resolved another successful investment, went off to spend the festive season with his beloved Edith.

However, there was one small difference on this occasion. It was one thing to commit a crime in a seaside town and attract the interest of the local press, but it was another matter to commit a crime in London where the national press would show interest. An article on the case in the *News of the World* attracted the attention of a Mr Haynes in Blackpool who spoke to his friend Mr Crossley, Smith's former landlord, who was still smarting over the callousness of Smith's attitude towards his wife's death. The report also attracted the attention of Mr Charles Burnham, Alice's father, who was intrigued with the similarities between the death of his daughter and the unfortunate lady found drowned in a bath at Highgate.

When Smith arrived at the solicitor's, armed with the paperwork to prove his right to Margaret Lofty's estate, he was told the legalities would take a little time. When he returned on 1 February, he was met by Detective Inspector Neil who arrested him on the simple charge of falsifying an entry on a marriage certificate. Then began the process of untangling the complexities of Smith's movements and 'marriages'. Unlike today, Inspector Neil was able to hold Smith while making inquiries into his background. Within three days he was charged with murder.

Smith's trial lasted nine days. The eminent defending counsel, Mr E. Marshall Hall KC, could do little in the face of the evidence to get his client off. Sir Bernard Spilsbury, the pathologist, gave evidence as to how he thought Smith had killed his victims, by grasping the ankles and pulling the legs up, causing the head to slide under the water. He even demonstrated the technique to the jury, using a volunteer nurse as the victim. In his enthusiasm he pulled her legs away so quickly that she was completely immersed and took in so much water she had to be given artificial respiration. Sitting in the dock scowling and shouting at witnesses and prosecutors, pleading his innocence, Smith had little effect on the jury who took just twenty-two minutes to bring in a verdict of guilty.

Smith's indifference to the death sentence when it was pronounced belied his inner fears. Committed to the condemned cell of Maidstone Prison, he at first rejected the Bible and the Prayer Book, ordering the warders to remove them and suggesting they should be sent to the detectives at Scotland Yard, who he felt would gain more benefit from reading them.

His bluster was not so obvious when he went to the gallows on 13 August 1915. He was whining in terror as John Ellis, the public executioner, took him to the scaffold to meet his fate.

13

A STAINED MATCHSTICK

The assistant at 'Staines', a cooking-equipment shop in London's Victoria Street, thought nothing of the sale of a chef's knife with a 10-inch blade to the well-dressed man with the clipped military moustache. It was after all just another transaction in the course of a Thursday morning, which was not an especially busy day for selling kitchen paraphernalia. The assistant wrapped the purchase, passed it over the counter, rang up the till, thanked the man for his custom, and watched him leave the shop. The customer, with the small parcel held tightly in his hand, walked briskly down Victoria Street, and crossed over into Vauxhall Bridge Road, where he was soon lost in the crowd.

Mr Judd was standing at the bar of the Blueboy public house, having an early lunch and thinking that there was nothing in particular that he had to do that afternoon. He felt a tap on his shoulder, turned and saw John, a man whom he often had a drink with. They talked for a while, and after some thirty minutes they left together and walked off along Rochester Row where they entered a block of offices at number 86 and climbed the stairs to the second floor. Moments later the two

men could be seen struggling down the stairs, carrying with
some difficulty a large, heavy, black leather trunk. Having
deposited it in the passage leading to the entrance, Mr Judd
bade his friend goodbye and walked back to his office.

At about 1.15pm, on Friday 6 May 1927, Mr Waller was
driving his cab along Pall Mall towards St James's Street,
when he was hailed by two men outside the Royal
Automobile Club. They asked to be taken to Rochester Row
Police Court. Upon arrival, they paid the fare and disappeared up the stairs into the court, where they were to answer
a motoring summons. As Waller made to pull away, he saw a
man with a moustache hailing him from across the street. So,
making a 'U'-turn Waller stopped his cab outside number 86
whereupon the man asked him for some help with a large
black trunk. Waller, gripping one of the handles, heaved
upwards and was so surprised by the weight of the trunk that
he immediately dropped it.

'Blimey, guv'nor, that's heavy. Is it full of money?'

The man told him to be careful, and together they carried
it across the pavement and put it in the space beside the
driver's seat.

'Where to?'

'Charing Cross railway station.'

When the cab arrived at the station, the passenger called
over a porter who pulled the trunk from the luggage platform
beside the driver. He too was surprised at the weight, and in
trying to obtain a purchase to drag it on to his porters' barrow he tore a piece off the end binding. He also remarked
about the weight and was told that the trunk was full of
books. Having loaded it on to his barrow the porter took it to
the Left-Luggage Office, where he dumped it down. He
accepted a tip from the man, who he noticed was of a military
appearance with a clipped moustache, and went off in search
of another customer. The military man, having waited for the
receipt to be completed, hurried out of the station and
climbed into a cab on the rank, directing the driver to take

him to Rochester Row, where he had just come from. He crumpled the left-luggage receipt and threw it out of the window.

A licensed bootblack, standing at his pitch on the pavement near the entrance to the forecourt of Charing Cross Station, saw the piece of paper arc out of the window of the cab and drop at his feet. Picking it up and unrolling it, he found that it was a receipt for a trunk. Being a man of tidy habits, he put it in his pocket intending to hand it in later that day. But he forgot, or so he said later in his statement.

Mr Glass, the head attendant at the Cloakroom and Left Luggage Office, Charing Cross station was not a happy man. Over the weekend a strange smell had started to pervade the room where the luggage was kept, and by Tuesday 10 May he was determined to find the cause of the offensive aroma that assailed his nostrils. His persistent search led him to a large black, leather-covered, wickerwork trunk. It was fastened with a heavy brass lock, and doubly secured with thick leather straps, and there were large gold-coloured 'A's painted at both ends. The label showed that it belonged to Mr F. Austin of St Leonards-on-Sea. Mr Glass was not to be deterred by the lock, and anyhow he could not contemplate sending such a foul-smelling container on a train. Using a jemmy, he prised open the brasswork to see what was inside.

Detective Inspector Steel was sitting in his office at Bow Street when the telephone rang. It was nearly one o'clock and time for lunch. The excitement and urgency of the voice on the phone caused him to forgo any intention of dining, and leaving his office he set out for Charing Cross Railway Station. What he saw in the left-luggage storeroom made him decide to contact the Chief Constable of Detectives at New Scotland Yard, who, when he heard what had been found, sent Chief Inspector Cornish to investigate.

Arriving at the station some thirty minutes later, the chief inspector's nose confirmed what he had already been told, and he ordered the immediate removal of the trunk to the public mortuary at Horseferry Road, not so very far from where it had originated four days previously.

The investigation of a murder had begun.

On the morning of Wednesday 11 May, Sir Bernard Spilsbury, the Home Office pathologist, began his examination of the trunk and its contents. The body it contained was that of a woman aged about thirty-five years, short and stout, with fashionably bobbed brown hair. The body had been divided into five parts, by amputation at the hip and shoulder joints. The legs and arms were wrapped in separate brown-paper parcels tied with string; an unsuccessful attempt had been made to remove the head, and this was wrapped in a cloth duster. Spilsbury found that there were bruises on the temple, the neck, and the abdomen, and concluded that death was due to asphyxia, caused by pressure over the mouth and the nostrils, while the victim had been in an unconscious state.

The torso was wrapped in woman's clothing, while other items of dress, and a pillow, had been used as packing. The collection in the trunk was completed with a pair of shoes, a handbag, some underwear, and a knitted jumper bearing a tag with the name P. Holt on it. Two laundry marks, the numbers 581 and 447, were discovered. All these items were handed to Cornish, who began the task of unravelling the mystery. Because the duster was stiff with dried blood, he did not look too closely at it; if he had done so, he would have seen that on the hem in one of the corners, the name of a hotel was embroidered.

The following morning, having checked the laundry marks – which revealed nothing – Cornish, accompanied by Steel, knocked on the door of a house in Tregunter Road, Kensington, the home of a Mr and Mrs Holt. Surprised at seeing the detectives on their doorstep, they looked carefully at the items they were shown and identified them as belonging to a Mrs Roles who had once been employed by them as a cook. They had no idea as to her present whereabouts.

The next task was to try and find where Mrs Roles had moved to. This did not prove to be too difficult, with help from the electoral register. They first located a Mr Roles, living at 82, Finborough Road, Fulham. It transpired that 'Mrs Roles' was not his wife. The detectives learnt that the couple had lived together for some time then parted, whereupon the woman used Mr Roles's surname to obtain employment. Her real name was Minni Alice Bonati, and she was separated from her husband who was an Italian waiter.

Again, luck was with the detectives and Mr Bonati was soon found, working at a restaurant in Chelsea. He told them how she had left him because she enjoyed the company of other men, and was working as a prostitute somewhere around Victoria Station. He had last seen her on 4 May at about four o'clock in the afternoon, in Sydney Street, Chelsea. Further inquiries showed that she rented a room in a house close by in Limerston Street, but a search of the premises revealed nothing. A neighbour stated that she hadn't been seen for some days.

Cornish called a conference of his team, and it was decided to release to the press a photograph of the trunk, in the hope that someone would recognise it. It was the first occasion that the police asked the press to publish photographs of items relating to a crime, which were to lead to the arrest of the murderer.

On the first day of publication, witnesses started to come forward. A dealer in second-hand luggage named Ward, who had a shop in the Brixton Road, told Steel that he had sold a trunk to a 'distinguished and military-looking man'. He thought that he had sold it on either 5 or 6 May, he wasn't sure which, but he remembered the man was very particular about the price and the size. The trunk had previously belonged to a family called Austin, who lived at St Leonards-on-Sea, near Hastings. Ward remembered that the purchaser left the shop with the trunk on his shoulders. At the time Ward thought this was rather strange, but the man had told him that he lived just up the road so it seemed that he had not far to carry it.

A bus conductor on the service that ran between Brixton Road and Victoria recalled helping a man to board, who was carrying a large black trunk. He had climbed on the bus near Mr Ward's shop, and had alighted in Vauxhall Bridge Road, close to Rochester Row. The conductor also had the impression that the man had a military background because of the way he looked, and his bearing.

The shoeblack then came forward and produced the left-luggage receipt, which showed that the trunk had been deposited at around 1.30pm on Friday 6 May. He explained how he had seen the docket being thrown from the window of a cab.

The porter was interviewed and gave a description of the suspect which tallied with the others. He also identified the trunk from the piece of binding he had accidentally pulled off.

The search was now on for any cab drivers who had either picked up a fare with a trunk in Rochester Row, or at Charing Cross Station for a destination in Rochester Row, at around the time stated on the left-luggage receipt.

The next piece of the jig-saw was fitted into place on Monday 16 May, when Mr Waller, after reading an account of the murder in a Sunday newspaper that had been left in his cab, contacted the police. He not only remembered the trunk and the man with it, but he could state exactly where he had picked up the said fare.

Cornish now knew where the trunk had come from, and where it had been taken to. The mystery was where it had been in the meantime, and who had put the body in it. It was certain that the suspect lived or worked in Rochester Row, and that he was a man of medium height and build, with a dark complexion, a moustache, and a decidedly military air. Cornish mused on who he could be. London was full of military types.

The detectives, armed with search warrants, now

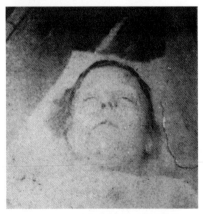

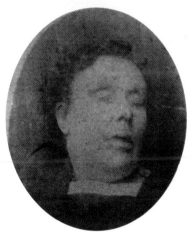

CHAPTER 8

Top Whitechapel Rd circa 1888

Centre Left Polly Nichols

Centre Right Annie Chapman

Left Elizabeth Stride

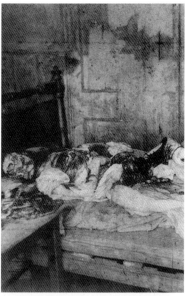

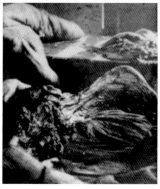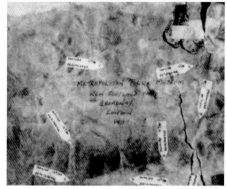

Top Left Catherine Eddowes

Top Right Mary Jane Kelly

Bottom Left View of Mary Jane Kelly's body.

Bottom Right The envelope postmarked Croydon sent to the museum containing lost letters and reports.

Opposite The 'Dear Boss' letter returned to the museum in 1988.

25 Sept: 1888.

Dear Boss

I keep on hearing the police
have caught me but they wont fix
me just yet. I have laughed when
they look so clever and talk about
being on the right track. That joke
about Leather apron gave me real
fits. I am down on whores and
I shant quit ripping them till I
do get buckled. Grand work the last
job was. I gave the lady no time to
squeal. How can they catch me
now. I love my work and want to start
again. You will soon hear of me
with my funny little games. I
saved some of the proper red stuff in
a ginger beer bottle over the last job
to write with but it went thick
like glue and I cant use it. Red
ink is fit enough I hope ha. ha.
The next job I do I shall clip
the lady's ears off and send to the
police officers just for jolly wouldnt
you. Keep this letter back till I
do a bit more work, then give
it out straight. My knife's so nice
and sharp I want to get to work
right away if I get a chance.
Good luck.

        yours truly

           Jack the Ripper

Dont mind me giving the trade name

CHAPTER 9

Top Left Albert Milsom. His alias is printed on the wall behind him.

Top Right Henry Fowler. The photographs were taken with a mirror behind, to provide a profile of the subject.

Bottom The lamp and wick which were found at the scene, and provided the main clue connecting Milsom and Fowler with the murder.

Left The tools used to break in and later found buried in the garden.

Below The ropes used to hang Milsom and Fowler. William Seaman was hanged in between them to prevent them from fighting on the scaffold. The rope in the centre of the picture would have been the next rope to be used had there been another execution. Capital punishment was abolished in 1969.

CHAPTER 10

Top Left Superintendent W Jenkins, the officer in charge of 'N' Division who wrote the report on the Tottenham outrage.

Top Right The car which was used to carry the wages.

Bottom Tottenham Police Station 1910.

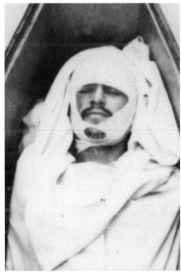

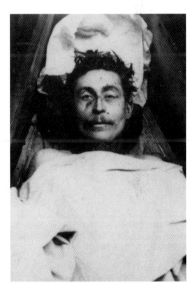

Top Left Front page of the *Daily Mirror* showing those killed and injured in the chase.

Top Right PC William F Tyler killed when confronting Hefeld.

Above Left Paul Hefeld.

Above Right Jacob Lepidus.

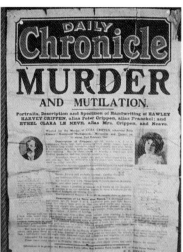

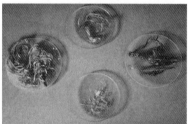

CHAPTER 11

Top Left Dr Hawley Harvey Crippen.

Top Right Murder poster showing samples of both Crippen and Le Neve's handwriting.

Centre Left Samples of Cora Crippen's hair with the Munt curlers found in the basement grave at 39 Hilldrop Crescent.

Centre Right The label on the pyjama jacket, a crucial piece of evidence in proving the case against Crippen

Left Captain Kendall.

Form No. 1.—400. 19/10/07. *This was the first message to be sent by Wireless*

Sent date _____

The MARCONI INTERNATIONAL MARINE COMMUNICATION COMPANY, Ltd.

WATERGATE HOUSE, YORK BUILDINGS, ADELPHI, LONDON, W.C.

No. 1

OFFICE   190

Prefix:	Code	Words		CHARGES TO PAY.
			Marconi Charge	
Office of Origin			Other Line Charge	
Service Instructions *Send to*			Delivery Charge	
			Total	

Brookhaven 3.30 pm
July 22nd

	Office sent to	Time sent	By whom sent

READ THE CONDITIONS PRINTED ON THE BACK OF THE FORM.

To: *Piers Liverpool*
3 pm GMT Friday 130 miles west Lizard
have strong suspicions that Crippen London
cellar murderer and accomplice are among saloon
passengers moustache taken off growing beard
accomplice dressed as boy voice manner and build
undoubtedly a girl both travelling as Mr
and Master Robinson

PLEASE ASK FOR OFFICIAL RECEIPT.

THE ACCUSED SPEAKS HIS SOLIC...

A "MORNING LEADER" ARTIST'S SKETCHES IN COURT

Top One of the telegrams sent back from the *SS Montrose* by the new wireless telegraph, to inform police that Dr Crippen and Ethel Le Neve were on board.

Bottom Left Crippen accompanied by Chief Inspector Dew being escorted off the ship that brought him back to England to stand trial.

Bottom Right Artists drawing of Crippen and Le Neve in the dock at Bow Street Magistrates Court, when being committed for trial at the Old Bailey.

CHAPTER 12

Left George Joseph Smith and Bessie Mundy.

Below The bath in which he drowned Margaret Lofty.

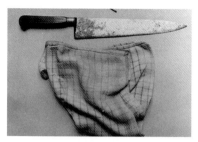

CHAPTER 13

Top Left Knife used by Robinson to dismember the body of Minnie Alice Bonetti. The duster was found in the trunk wrapped around the head. The name Greyhound in the corner, led to Robinson's arrest.

Top Right The trunk in which the body of Bonetti was found at Charing Cross railway station.

Bottom Police examining the trunk and other articles.

CHAPTER 14

Top Left John George Haigh.

Top Right Gall stones and a foot reconstructed from bones found at the scene.

Bottom Items in the Haigh case. The 40 gallon oil drums used to dissolve the bodies. The gun used to shoot his victims. The remains of the handbag. His gas mask and riding mac.

Top Left Police officer dressed in the clothing worn by Haigh when disposing of Mrs Durand Deacon's body.

CHAPTER 15

Top Right John Reginald Halliday Christie and his wife.

Bottom Left 10 Rillington Place.

Bottom Right The front door and window of the living room, where Mrs Christie was found under the floorboards.

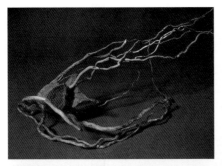

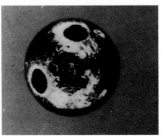

Top Left Thoracic vertebrae of Ruth Fuerst with a root growing through it. The rate of growth of the root determined the period of time that the body had been buried.

Top Right Cupboard which contained three bodies.

CHAPTER 16

Second Left Newspaper headline.

Third Left Scanning Electron Microscope Mount with the pellet set on the top.

Bottom Left The pellet showing the holes which were filled with the poison ricin. The pellet is only 1.53 mm in diameter and is smaller than a pinhead.

CHAPTER 17

Top Left Dennis Nilsen.

Top Right 23 Cranley Gardens.

Bottom Bathroom where parts of the body were found.

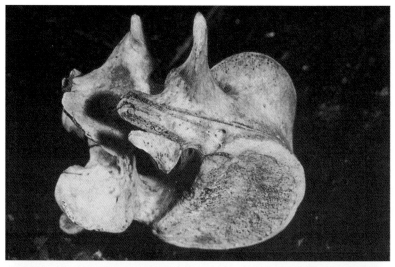

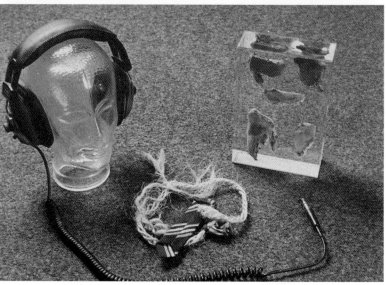

Top Vertebrae with saw marks when body was dismembered.

Bottom Earphones and tie reinforced with string, used to strangle victims. Body samples (right in picture) removed from the drain.

descended on the block of offices opposite Rochester Row
Police Station. These were occupied by a number of different
concerns, so that more than eighty people employed in the
building were interviewed. Some had seen the trunk in the
hall when they had left the building for lunch, and noticed
that it had gone when they returned. Others noticed nothing
out of the ordinary.

An office on the second floor occupied by a company calling itself 'Edward and Co., Business Transfer Agents'
attracted the attention of Cornish. It was a sparsely furnished
office, with a table and some chairs; a typewriter and filing
cabinets; a wastepaper basket; and some ashtrays. The floor
was covered with a threadbare square of Axminster carpet. A
check at Somerset House showed that the name had not been
entered on the Business Names Register. The company who
owned the building were able to tell the police that the office
had been rented by a Mr John Robinson, and that he had sent
them a letter dated 9 May terminating his tenancy, and asking that the typewriter be returned to the company that had
supplied it. He had paid his rent arrears with a cheque drawn
on the Westminster Bank, who in turn gave his address as De
Laune Street in Kennington.

Cornish now felt he was getting somewhere but when the
detectives arrived at the house, the landlady told them that
Robinson had left saying he was going to Lancashire. The
only thing she could help them with was a telegram which
had been returned to sender marked 'address unknown'.
Opening it, they found that it had been sent by Robinson to
his wife at a small hotel in Hammersmith called The
Greyhound.

Cornish switched his attentions to this new location.
There was little difficulty in finding the woman he was looking for. Not only did Mrs Robinson live there, she also
worked there. The telegram had proved to be a stroke of
good luck. When delivered, it had been handed to a newly
employed barmaid who was not aware that Mrs Robinson

was an employee, and so she handed it back to the telegraph boy. When questioned Mrs Robinson revealed that she was separated from her husband, but that she kept in contact with him. Would she help?

Then there was a further development. Detective Seymour, who was working at Kennington on another case, knocked at the door of 26, New Street, Kennington, and found that another Mrs Robinson lived there. On questioning the woman about her name, he discovered that she not only knew the wanted man, she was married to him! So there appeared to be two Mrs Robinsons. Did this indicate bigamy?

The real Mrs Robinson, the one working at The Greyhound, was not at all pleased when she heard the news of her husband's infidelity, and the aggrieved woman readily agreed to help the police. A meeting was arranged for 7pm on Thursday 19 May, at the Elephant and Castle public house at Walworth. Cornish was obliged to wait another forty-eight hours before he could meet his prime suspect, but the puzzle was slowly fitting into place.

Meanwhile other inquiries were progressing. The initial searches made at the Rochester Row office had revealed nothing, so it was decided that a more detailed examination should be carried out. This task was given to Detective Sergeant Burt (later to become head of the Special Branch) and Detective Sergeant Clarke.

The office had been meticulously cleaned. They found that a fender bar on the fire was loose, and a window pane was cracked, otherwise everything was in order. There was nothing in the files, nothing in the fireplace. Clarke looked at the wickerwork wastepaper basket. It appeared to contain only cigarette ends and matches, apparently emptied from the ashtray. He tipped them on to the table, and checked each one. No clues. He looked at the basket again, lifting it up to the light, and saw that something was caught in the weave. It was a matchstick, just two inches long. Clarke retrieved it and saw that it was tinged with a brown stain. Could it be dried blood? Was this the clue they had been looking for, the one that would link the office with the murder? Clarke carefully put the match in an envelope, and continued looking for more evidence.

Robinson walked into the Elephant and Castle at ten past seven on 19 May and was immediately approached by Cornish and Steel. Robinson did not seem at all perturbed when told they were police officers investigating a serious crime. He agreed to accompany them to the Yard to assist them in their inquiries, and when there he readily agreed to take part in an identification parade.

Three people – Ward, Waller and the railway porter failed to pick him out from the line-up. He was questioned but gave very plausible answers, denying all knowledge of Mrs Bonati and of the trunk. In the absence of any positive proof to link him with the murder, he had to be released.

Cornish thought long and hard. If this was not their man, who could it be? He was certain that he had the right man. But where was the evidence? How could he prove murder against him? The questions flooded his mind, and then there came a breakthrough.

The scientists had been examining the matchstick and the duster. The duster, which had been wrapped around Mrs Bonati's head, had been treated and the hotel name in the corner that had not been spotted earlier now showed up clearly. The name was 'Greyhound', the hotel in Hammersmith where the police had located Mrs Robinson. Later, a Miss Moore who had been Robinson's typist was able to tell the court that she had seen her employer using the duster in the office; it had been brought there by his wife, when she visited the office.

Not only was this good news for the investigators but there was the second piece of evidence – the matchstick. A test had shown that the brown stain was in fact blood. The science of blood testing was in its infancy in those days, but there was enough known about grouping to make accurate tests. When the blood on the match was compared with that of Minni Bonati, they were found to be of the same group.

Now there were direct links between Robinson, the trunk and the Greyhound Hotel. Also, more importantly, there was a link between Mrs Bonati and the office at Rochester Row.

On the following Monday morning Detective Sergeants Clarke and Seymour went to De Laune Street, where they were admitted to the house by the landlady and shown up to Robinson's room. Finding the door open they went in. The suspect awoke to find the two detectives standing over him.

'Get dressed. We want you to accompany us for further questioning in connection with the murder of Mrs Bonati.'

Their tone was hard, and it made Robinson fearful. He was taken to the Yard where he was put into the detention room. Clarke noticed that he was becoming agitated and nervy, and it was decided to leave him alone for a while to give him a chance to think. After an hour he knocked on the detention-room door. When Clarke answered it, Robinson asked to see Chief Inspector Cornish. When asked why, he replied, 'I want to tell him all about it.'

Cornish cautioned the suspect and he started to make his statement. He said that he had been accosted outside his office by Mrs Bonati on 4 May, and that he took her up to his office where she became abusive because he would not give her a pound note. She went to pick something up from the fireplace and he hit her in the face. She fell backwards and struck her head on a chair. He didn't know what to do, so he cut her up to get rid of her. When asked about the knife, he said he had buried it on Clapham Common, from where it was recovered later.

Robinson was charged with murder and the trial began at the Old Bailey on Monday 11 July. The judge was Mr Justice Swift. Mr Percival Clarke and Mr Christmas Humphries appeared for the prosecution, and Mr Lawrence Vine led for the defence. The point at issue at the trial was whether the death of Mrs Bonati was an accident or intentional. Robinson gave evidence in which he more or less admitted everything he had done, but claimed that he did not have any intention of killing her.

Spilsbury's evidence conflicted with this – he was up against an old pathology adversary, Dr Bronte, who appeared for the defence. Bronte was not able to disprove the prosecution's contention that Mrs Bonati had been suffocated while unconscious, probably with the cushion they found in the trunk.

On Wednesday 13 July, after a trial lasting three days, the ten men and two women on the jury brought in a verdict of guilty. Donning the black cap the judge pronounced sentence of death.

Robinson appealed, but the appeal was disallowed. So on Friday 12 August 1927, after leaving most of his possessions to his bigamous wife, prisoner 4364 was hanged at Pentonville Prison by Thomas William Pierrepoint. The final part of the jig-saw had been fitted into place.

14

THE ACID BATH MURDERER

It is very easy to commit a murder. It is very difficult to dispose of the body. Premeditation allows time for the murderer to contemplate the problems before committing the act, and there are many diverse options for consideration.

How do you kill the intended victim? By shooting, stabbing, strangling, drowning, or poisoning?

How do you get rid of the cadaver? Should you burn it, bury it, maybe drop it into the sea? Would it be better to dump it in some inaccessible place where it may not be found?

All these methods have been tried. All have had their successes. Most have been discovered.

John George Haigh contemplated the problem, and came up with what he thought would be a foolproof method. He would dissolve the bodies of his victims in acid. No body. No trace. No evidence against him.

Haigh lived as a paying guest at the Onslow Court Hotel, Queen's Gate, London. Other residents, who were too polite to ask, had the impression that he was a company director who to all appearances seemed to do very well for himself. He was always immaculately dressed, favouring browns and greys for his suits, with matching red ties, and able to afford a smart dark crimson Alvis saloon to drive around in.

Those who lived in the same hotel, mainly elderly ladies, found that he had an abundance of charm, and was always ready to pass the time of day, or sit and listen to their trivial gossip over dinner. Mrs Durand Deacon was one of those who enjoyed his company, and knowing that he had some involvement in patenting new ideas, confided in him about her interest in manufacturing disposable plastic stick-on fingernails. When she showed him what she had in mind, using pieces of thick brown paper and glue to demonstrate, he became quite absorbed with the idea. He asked her to give him a few days to think about the problem, and he would work out a way of making them.

He certainly thought about the problem. He contacted a friend and asked him to order some carboys of sulphuric acid for a process he was working on in his workshop at Leopold Road in Crawley. He also purchased a forty-gallon steel oil drum, which had been treated to withstand acid, and he visited an army-surplus store where he bought an old stirrup pump.

A few days later Haigh came into the hotel dining room where Mrs Durand Deacon was lunching by herself, and suggested she might like to visit his workshop in Crawley to see what progress he was making with her idea. She accepted willingly, and he agreed to pick her up the following day in the early afternoon. After all it was not every day that she had the opportunity of having a run in a rather exclusive car, with a rather charming gentleman.

No one saw her leave the hotel in Queen's Gate, but she was observed later that day, around 4.15pm, by a receptionist, coming out of the ladies' room at the George Hotel in Crawley. That would be the last time anyone saw Olive Durand Deacon alive. The hotel receptionist watched as the woman in the black coat climbed into a dark red Alvis parked at the front of the hotel. The car was driven off by a neat-looking man with a moustache. Haigh did not have to drive too far, just around the corner to the yard of his tiny workshop, where he carefully closed the gates and politely opened the car door, helped Mrs Durand Deacon out, and ushered her into the fateful room.

She was looking around the rather dingy interior when Haigh drew her attention to some samples of material displayed on a bench. As she bent over to examine them, he quietly pulled out a .38 Enfield service revolver, and holding it to the back of her head, he pulled the trigger. A convulsive jerk, and the body crumpled to the floor.

It was about 4.30pm on Friday 18 February 1949. It had taken just four days from the time that the poor lady had suggested the fingernails idea to Haigh, to the moment of her death.

At the time Mrs Durand Deacon first imparted her novel idea to Haigh, the latter was deeply in debt. A man with champagne tastes and only beer money to pay for them, he had run up gambling debts, was overdrawn at the bank, and the hotel manager was becoming impatient over his unpaid bill. Haigh saw the opportunity of profit from letting Mrs Durand Deacon believe that he was interested in setting up a business partnership with her. He had noticed that she wore expensive clothes, and certainly the glitter of her jewellery suggested money and not penury.

Immediately after shooting Mrs Durand Deacon, Haigh set about creating an alibi. Leaving her where she lay, he jumped into his car and went off to visit an old contact to whom he owed money, and who worked not too far away. On entering the contact's office, Haigh made a point of stressing the time – it was 4.45pm. Some small talk, and a promise to pay back his debt, then he left and drove straight back to Leopold Road. He had completed the first part of his preconceived plan. Now came the second part.

First he removed the Persian lamb coat from Mrs Durand Deacon's body. Then he methodically removed her jewellery:

rings, necklace, watch, and earrings. He picked up her red plastic handbag and rifled through its contents, taking anything he could use, sell or pawn. Then he laid the oil drum on its side and rolled it towards where the body lay and began to heave the dead weight of the corpse into it. It was not easy. First the head and arms, and then the torso and legs were unceremoniously crammed into the container. It took all Haigh's strength to heave the drum upright with the body in it, and still more effort to compress the body more tightly into it. He picked up the odd items lying around: shoes and handbag, and dropped them in with the body. Taking off his jacket and shoes, he pulled on a pair of rubber boots and donned a rubberised light brown riding mac, followed by a black rubber apron. He then pulled on a service respirator, the type that had been issued to soldiers during the war. A pair of thick rubber gloves completed the macabre attire.

Haigh rolled one of the glass carboys of concentrated sulphuric acid alongside the drum, removed the stopper, and fed the pipe from the stirrup pump into it. He put the other end into the drum and started to pump. Acid began slowly to trickle on to the body. As it bit into the tissue, acrid fumes rose, but they did not bother Haigh. His gas mask prevented them from entering his nostrils.

Having emptied one carboy he opened another and repeated the process. The acid became more agitated as it burnt away the body, spitting and spluttering as the water in the body was converted to steam. Haigh pumped in more, and still more, of the oily corrosive fluid.

Slowly, what was left of the disintegrating body sank beneath the surface of the steaming pink-tinged, bubbling liquid. He saw what was left of her red plastic handbag shoot up to the surface, and then disappear back into the seething porridge of death. When it came up again he grabbed it with his gloved hands, and not knowing what to do with it, went outside and threw it on to a pile of waste at the back of the workshop.

By 6.30pm, he was somewhat tired from his exertions, and

decided that a snack would help. He removed his gruesome clothing and drove off to Ye Olde Ancient Priors café, where he ordered tea and poached egg on toast, paying with money he had found in Mrs Durand Deacon's handbag. Temporarily replete, he returned to Leopold Road and completed his grisly task, finally placing a lid on the drum. He put the Persian lamb coat in the car, the jewellery in a box, turned out the lights, and locked up. He decided that a proper meal was in order, so he went to the George Hotel, where he ordered the best dinner that the restrictions of post-war rationing would allow. Strange how killing can make you hungry. It is the body reacting to the stimulation of an increased flow of adrenalin.

By no means was this Haigh's first experience of murder. In 1944 he had met an old acquaintance, William Donald McSwann, in the Goat Tavern, in Kensington High Street. They had downed a few drinks and he had taken McSwann back to his basement flat in Gloucester Road. There he killed him, disposing of the body by dissolving it in acid, then pouring what was left down the drain. He had maintained contact with Mr and Mrs McSwann, William's parents, convincing them by a series of forged letters that their son was still alive, but had gone to ground to avoid being called up into the services. A year later Haigh inveigled them to his flat, shot them, and disposed of their bodies by the same method. Then posing as their son, he forged documents to show that he was the sole heir to their estate, and so inherited £5600.

In 1947 he met Dr and Mrs Henderson, and persuaded them to visit his little workshop at Crawley. Again he shot them, and disposed of them with his tried and tested acid method. His bank balance increased by a further £7700 over this period, as the result of the sale of the Hendersons' assets.

Like all those who are involved in crime, success breeds confidence, and after killing his last victim, Haigh was more than confident.

On the Saturday following his murder of Mrs Durand

Deacon, first he went to Putney where he sold one of her rings, then to Horsham to visit Bull's the jewellers. Here he asked for a valuation of several pieces of the late Mrs Durand Deacon's jewellery. He now returned to Crawley to see how the acid was working, then went to a dry cleaners in Reigate to have the coat cleaned.

When he returned to the hotel he found general concern about the missing resident, but Haigh was not too bothered. He had raised enough money to pay off his hotel bill and keep his creditors from the door.

By Sunday the staff at the hotel, and in particular Mrs Lane, a close friend of Mrs Durand Deacon, were really worried by her absence. Mrs Lane told Haigh that her friend had told her she was going with him to his factory in Crawley. He denied the visit had taken place, saying she had not turned up at the place where they had arranged to meet. The first wave had rippled the surface of his confidence. It was about to become a very stormy sea.

Haigh suggested that they should inform the police of Mrs Durand Deacon's disappearance. Gentleman to the last, he offered to drive Mrs Lane to Chelsea Police Station.

Woman Detective Sergeant Lambourne interviewed the two and listened to their story. Her curiosity was aroused by this concerned old lady and her rather suave companion who spoke with the slightest hint of a Yorkshire accent. He would interject while Mrs Lane was talking, qualifying a point here and adding one there. She politely listened and gently questioned, and entered all the facts in the Missing Persons Register.

When they left, Sergeant Lambourne's female intuition told her that Mr Haigh was not quite what he appeared to be. She had a feeling that there was something more to this, so she went to the hotel in Queen's Gate and spoke to the manager. She was interested in what he told her, particularly the fact that Haigh had at long last paid off his long-standing hotel bill. She looked at room 115, where Mrs Durand Deacon had lived, spoke to the chambermaid, and left.

Sergeant Lambourne decided to consult the Register of Criminals, first set up in 1758. She put in a request to the Criminal Record office and on receipt of the file found some intriguing information. She went to see her Divisional Detective Inspector, Shelley Symes.

Monday was another busy day for Haigh. He went back to Crawley to see what was happening in the acid bath. He removed the lid and found the drum was half filled with quiescent acid sludge which included the skeletal frame. On the top there was a two-inch scum of body fat.

Acid will not quickly dissolve body fat. Haigh scooped this off into a bucket, and dumped it on the waste ground at the back of the workshop. Then he removed as much of the liquid and sludge as he could, and pumped in fresh acid to dissolve the bones. Satisfied with his labours he then went to Horsham, where he again visited Bull's the jewellers and collected the valuation. He visited a friend to whom he owed £50, and made a promise to pay him, and then he went back to the Onslow Court Hotel. Waiting for him were Inspector Symes and his Detective Inspector Albert Webb, who questioned him about the disappearance of the elderly lady with the Persian lamb coat. Haigh made a statement and they left him confidently believing that he had managed to convince them that he was as mystified as they were and had no knowledge of her whereabouts.

Later that week he returned to Horsham and offered the jewellery to the valuers, who bought it for cash; he paid off some more of his debts, and returned to examine the drum. Now he found that there was little but liquid and sludge, the bones had at long last dissolved. He wheeled the drum outside to the back of his workshop, tipped it over, and what was left of Mrs Durand Deacon was committed to the earth.

Haigh soon realised that the police were showing an unhealthy interest in his movements, and he was trying to get rid of everything that could point to him as being involved in

Mrs Durand Deacon's disappearance. After all he had got rid
of the body, and if there was no body and nothing to connect
him with it, how could the plodding police prove anything
against him? He had dealt with the Hendersons and the
McSwanns in the same way and he had not been caught, so
why should this case be different?

But there were still two vital pieces of evidence to dispose
of: the gun, and a lot of papers relating to his latest victim's
business affairs and accounts. These were lying in a box in
the boot of his car. Haigh now panicked a little. The police
had already inspected his workshop and so, assuming they
would not return, he stupidly concealed the gun and the
papers under some junk at the back of his premises. Detective
Sergeant Pat Heslin of the Sussex CID, in his pursuit of
information regarding Mrs Durand Deacon's disappearance,
decided he would return and have another look at the little
workshop in Leopold Road. He contacted the owner of the
premises, and with his permission they forced the lock. It
did not take long to find the box, filled with the incriminating
papers and the weapon. Also, there was a receipt tucked away
in a ration book. It was for ten shillings – the price of having
a Persian lamb coat cleaned, issued by a shop at Reigate.

Professor Keith Simpson, the pathologist, went to the scene
and found something else. His keen eyes searching the rub-
bish on the tip at the back of the workshop spotted some
small pieces of what appeared to be gravel. They were human
gall stones, and like body fat they do not dissolve in acid.
Professor Simpson also found some small bones. These had
been covered in body fat, which had protected them from
being dissolved in the acid. He then found an acrylic denture.
Acrylic is a man-made material developed during the Second
World War, and will withstand body enzymes and acids. It is
still the most common material used today for making den-
tures. Also discovered was the base and the handle of a red
plastic handbag, which had been in the drum during the
whole period of the dissolving process. There was also the

main body of the handbag, which had been so carelessly thrown away. This was the first time that it was realised just how resistant plastic can be to the action of acid.

Reconstruction of the small bones provided a foot which fitted into one of Mrs Durand Deacon's shoes, and a check on her dental records proved that the denture belonged to her.

Monday 28 February, was the day the storm broke for Haigh. He was arrested when he returned to the hotel and taken to Chelsea for questioning. Systematically, persistently, methodically, the questions were put to him about matters he had already revealed. He was asked about the contradictions in what he had said, and his replies were noted. He was re-examined on them and slowly the tangle of his conniving mind began to unravel, until weary of the mental battle he succumbed, and answered the one big question that was in everyone's mind.

'What have you done with Mrs Durand Deacon?'

The reply was equally succinct.

'I have dissolved her in acid.'

To a detective, this sort of short abrupt answer after hours of pitting your wits, trying to fit fact with fiction, lie with truth, causes a sharp intake of breath, followed by a slow exhalation. The eye contact with the suspect is broken, and you turn in mute amazement to whoever else is sitting near you and wonder whether you can believe what you are hearing. It is the moment of truth.

Haigh had one thing in mind now – how to prevent himself from being hanged. Ever the con man, he concocted a story about cutting the necks of his victims and drinking their blood. This was real sensationalism, so sensational in fact that the editor of the *Daily Mirror* made a headline story of it, and was sent to prison for contempt of court.

Why did Haigh make such a macabre statement? Was it to gratify his ego; to gain notoriety; to get publicity? It was none of these. He hoped it would help to prove he was suffering from insanity and, instead of receiving the death penalty, he would be sent to Broadmoor. Haigh was obviously not aware of the implications of his statement. If he had drunk human blood, it would probably have acted as an emetic and made him dreadfully sick.

The trial at Lewes Assizes was brief. It started on Monday 18 July and ended the following afternoon. Against thirty-three witnesses for the prosecution, there was only one for the defence. Maxwell Fyfe, KC, MP, Haigh's counsel, tried to demonstrate that his client was insane. There was little to convince the court. Haigh did not look like a man suffering from clinical insanity.

The jury were out for only seventeen minutes, and returned with a verdict of guilty. Haigh made an appeal but it was dismissed. He celebrated his fortieth birthday in the condemned cell.

The following details appear in Albert Pierrepoint's diary of executions:

Date	Aug 10 1949
Name	John George Haig
Age	40
Height	5 ft 9 in
Weight	150 lb
Drop	7 ft 4 in
Town	Wandsworth, London
Excutioner	A.P.H. Kirk

15

JOHN REGINALD HALLIDAY CHRISTIE

The house was at the end of a cul-de-sac, just one of a line of mean run-down terraced dwellings which had seen better days. It abutted on to the wall of a laundry from where a tall chimney constantly belched forth black grimy smoke, while behind the houses on the opposite side of the road, the clanking clattering trains of the Underground's Metropolitan line ran.

This was 10, Rillington Place in Notting Hill, where John Reginald Halliday Christie killed six women in a series of murders that left an indelible impression in the minds of the British public. In this depressing environment Christie lived with his wife Ethel, a quietly spoken woman to whom he had been married since 1920. She seldom if ever argued with him and she had long since become used to the strange moods that he was subject to. They had ceased to have intimate relationships within their marriage and she lived her life with a stoical acceptance of their threadbare existence. To make money to supplement what meagre allowances they could get from public welfare funds, Christie sub-let rooms in their rented house to anyone who found their decrepit accommodation acceptable.

Christie was not one of life's success stories. He had moved from one job to another working as a cinema projectionist, a clerk, or by taking any employment from which he could earn money. He seldom remained long in a job, usually telling his employers that his poor health prevented him from staying. The Second World War gave him a rare opportunity to gratify his ambition to achieve status and respect. He was able to join the police as a war reservist, managing to hide a number of convictions for petty crimes that he had committed in his early life.

Stationed at Harrow Road he carried out his duties efficiently enough, with a particular enthusiasm for catching people who were showing lights during the black-out. His work brought him into contact with numerous people including a young Austrian student nurse called Ruth Fuerst whom he met in August 1943. As his wife was away from home he invited her back to his flat where, according to the statement he made years later, they made love. While in the throes of passion he wrapped a piece of rope around her neck and strangled her. Because of his known inability to indulge in normal sexual relationships, it is more likely that he used the opportunity to test his newly devised method of killing by administering gas to her under the pretext that it would relax and increase her sexual libido. As his wife was due home the following day he concealed the body from her by first putting it under the floorboards, and then burying it in the garden when she went out shopping. That was the last anyone saw of Ruth Fuerst until her remains were dug up some ten years later.

In early 1944 he was required to resign from the police when he was caught *in flagrante delicto* by the husband of a member of the station canteen staff. The wartime shortage of available manpower ensured that he soon found other work getting employment as a clerk with a company in Acton. Here he met his second victim, Miss Muriel Eady. She often called on the Christies at their home and during one of her visits complained that she was suffering from a cold. Christie, never slow to impress on people the medical knowledge he had acquired at police first aid classes, offered a cure which she was quick to accept. Again waiting until his wife was absent, he invited Eady to the house and applied the mask of his gas machine to her face. Turning on the tap he watched the gas bubbling through a solution of Friar's Balsam, in a glass Kilner jar, the Balsam being a means of effectively disguising the odour of rotting vegetation given off by coal gas. Unconsciousness was followed by strangulation with one of her own stockings. It is certain that he then indulged in intercourse with the body either before or just after death. Again he disposed of the body by burying it in the garden, where it too remained concealed until disinterred nine years later.

The greatest number of murders to be investigated in a single inquiry in England were those of thirty-seven patrons of the Spanish Club, at 18, Denmark Place, London, on Saturday 16 August 1980. John Thompson, aged forty-two, annoyed because he thought he had been overcharged for a rum and coke, poured petrol through the letterbox and then threw in a lighted match. This caused a fireball to roar up the stairs to the top floor, incinerating those in the club. On 7 May 1981, Thompson was sentenced to life imprisonment.

An opportunity to indulge his desire for necrophilia again presented itself in 1949 when Beryl Evans, the wife of one of his tenants, asked him if he would terminate her pregnancy. One child was enough, she did not want another. Christie readily agreed. Persuading her to lie down on an eiderdown on the floor of an upstairs room, he administered the relaxing inhalant with his tried and tested gas jar. Having gratified his bizarre fetish he later connived with her husband Timothy Evans to dispose of the body. This was followed by the strangulation with Evans' fourteen-month-old baby daughter

Geraldine with a tie. Timothy Evans later made a statement confessing both murders and was finally put on trial for killing the baby girl. Christie quite blandly gave evidence at the trial, innocently denying any suggestions made by the defence that he could have been involved in the deaths of either Mrs Evans or the baby. The court was convinced and Evans, unable to convince the jury, was found guilty and sentenced to death. He was hanged at Pentonville on 9 March 1950. It was an execution that was to have repercussions years later when Christie also stood trial for murder.

So his life dragged along until in December 1952 he once again felt the desire to kill. This time the victim was his wife Ethel. Waking up in the night he found that she was suffering from a convulsion, so to relieve her of the pain he strangled her. The reason he later gave for causing her death was that as she suffered from arthritis and insomnia it saved her from further pain. The more sinister reason for her death was that she had become aware of Christie's activities and rather than run the risk of her disclosing them, he had simply decided to kill her. To maintain the idea that she was still alive, he began writing letters to her family explaining that she could not write because of rheumatism in her fingers. This prevented her from putting pen to paper. Having concealed her under the floorboards of the front room he again went about inveigling women to visit him.

As Ethel was dead he could now carry out his work without interruption, so he began to visit local cafés, where he met young women who were desperate to have abortions. He covertly began offering his services as an abortionist to some of these women, cajoling them with his soft voice and impressing them with his medical knowledge. They seemed to be quite overawed with his quiet personality and apparently oblivious to the dangers as they followed him to the house of death.

Between January and March 1953 he murdered three times in quick succession. In January he gassed and strangled Kathleen Moloney. Later in the same month he murdered

Rita Nelson in the same way, and in March he killed Hectorina McClennan. She unlike the others had only been searching for accommodation.

Christie placed each of the bodies in a cupboard in the kitchen one behind the other. Then he papered over the door. Being desperately short of money, he had begun to sell his furniture and possessions, and with what money he had made from the sale he walked away from 10, Rillington Place on the 19 March, leaving behind a tomb.

Mr Beresford Brown took up residence four days later and went into the kitchen to see what alterations were needed to make it habitable. He pulled back the paper that covered the door, and peeping through a crack, he saw the body of Hectorina McClennan sitting on a pile of ashes. Behind her was Miss Nelson and under her, Miss Moloney. When medically examined all of them had evidence of carbon monoxide poisoning; all had been strangled; all had evidence of sexual intercourse at around the time of death.

The police investigation opened with a man-hunt for Christie. A week went by. The house was examined in detail by detectives and forensic experts. The floorboards were raised and revealed the body of Mrs Christie. When the garden was dug up the bodies of Fuerst and Eady came to light but there was still no sign of the wanted man.

It was Tuesday 31 March at 11am when PC Ledger walking his beat at Putney, saw a man leaning over a wall gazing into the river near Putney Pier. Thinking that he looked similar to the wanted man he approached him and asked his name. He replied that he was John Waddington and lived at Westbourne Grove. Not convinced, Ledger asked him to remove his hat. The bald head and horn-rimmed glasses left no doubt that he had found the murderer wanted all over the country.

First he was taken to Putney Police Station and then to Notting Hill, where after questioning he was charged with the murder of his wife.

The trial began on 22 June in No 1 Court at the Old Bailey

in front of Mr Justice Finnemore. The prosecution was led by the Attorney General Sir Lionel Heald, and the defence was conducted by Mr Curtis Bennett QC. It lasted four days. Attempts by the defence to prove insanity failed and after retiring for eighty-five minutes the jury returned a verdict of guilty.

The mandatory death sentence followed and on 15 July at Pentonville Prison Christie walked to the scaffold.

It immediately raised the question as to whether Evans was innocent. An inquiry carried out by Mr John Scott Henderson QC after Christie had been charged, and who interviewed him as part of the inquiry, concluded that Evans was guilty of the murder of both his daughter and his wife. Another re-examination of the case was opened by Mr Justice Brabin in 1965. He concluded that it was more probable than not that Evans had killed his wife but not his daughter. As he had been convicted only for the murder of his daughter Evans was given a pardon in 1966. Christie always vehemently denied murdering Geraldine, but accepted that he killed Mrs Evans.

Today the houses in the street where it all took place have been pulled down and replaced with neat modern dwellings. The railway still clatters along parallel with the traffic that growls along the Westway. All there is to mark the site of the house is a space. There is one number missing. You can find number 9 and you can find number 11. You cannot find number 10.

16

GEORGI MARKOV

O n Thursday 7 September 1978, Georgi Ivanov Markov, a Bulgarian, was standing at a bus stop on the south side of Waterloo Bridge, when he felt a sharp blow in the back of his right thigh. As he turned round he saw a man bending down to pick up an umbrella from the pavement. The man, speaking according to Markov in an East European accent, apologised for his clumsiness and proceeded to flag down a passing taxi. Markov pondered as he saw the cab disappear over the bridge, but when his bus drew up, he climbed on board, paid his fare and for the moment forgot about the incident.

Georgi Markov was an interesting personality. He was an author and a playwright who had defected from his native country, Bulgaria, in 1969. His anti-communist views, which he projected in his writings, had made him an unpopular figure with the hierarchy of his country of origin, so he had come to England in 1971 and was presently working for the Bulgarian section of the BBC's World Service, at Bush House in the Aldwych. At the same time he had contracts to provide material for the CIA-backed Radio Free Europe, and Deutschwelle, the German propaganda service.

When he arrived at his office shortly after the incident, he complained to one of his colleagues that his right leg was extremely sore. When the site of the pain was examined, an angry red spot some four and a half centimetres in diameter was found. The area at the back of the thigh was very inflamed and appeared similar in appearance to a wasp or bee sting.

Markov worked throughout the afternoon, preparing scripts for transmission to his home country the following day, and that evening returned to his home near Clapham Common. He complained to his wife that he felt dizzy and weak, and as he had to rise early the next morning for a broadcast, he went to bed downstairs so as not to disturb her. In the early hours of the morning she heard him moving around, and upon going to investigate found that he had developed a high temperature and was feeling very nauseous. She called a doctor who diagnosed that he was suffering from some sort of viral infection, and that the best place for him was in bed. During the morning his condition worsened, and another examination showed that it was likely he was suffering from some sort of blood poisoning. Late that evening, at 11.15pm, he was admitted to St James' Hospital at Balham. By this time, some thirty-four hours after the Waterloo Bridge incident, Markov was a very sick man indeed.

The signs and symptoms that he had developed made it very difficult to diagnose exactly what was the matter with him. Blood tests were taken which showed that he had a slightly high white-cell count. This did not seem to represent an immediate problem, but the following day there was a marked deterioration in his condition. His blood pressure dropped, his pulse rate became erratic, and his temperature rose dramatically. A decision was made by the medical staff to move him to the Intensive Therapy Unit, where he could be kept under closer observation, and where his condition could be monitored.

Another blood test was taken, and it was found that his white-cell count had accelerated very considerably and his condition was critical. Despite every form of medical aid, on the following day, he became disorientated and began pulling drips out of his body. He suffered a cardiac arrest and at 10.40am life was declared extinct.

On the morning of Tuesday 12 September, Dr Rufus Crompton, the Senior Lecturer in Forensic Medicine at St George's Hospital Medical School, carried out an autopsy at Wandsworth Public Mortuary to determine the cause of death. Commander James Neville, head of New Scotland Yard's Anti-Terrorist Squad, attended and although there was doubt as to whether Markov had died from anything other than natural causes, he was taking no chances. He understood the phobias about clandestine attacks that were suffered by those who had defected, and he wanted to ensure that every aspect of this man's suspicious death was covered.

His fears were confirmed. Examination showed that the lymph glands, kidneys, liver, heart, all showed signs of capillary haemorrhaging. Numerous other disruptions were found in the body, and it was realised that this was no ordinary death. On the back of the right leg, the red spot had developed into a bruise, and it was decided to remove a sample of tissue from this area. This was taken to the Chemical Research Establishment at Porton, where a more detailed analysis of the wound could be carried out.

In the pathology laboratory, Dr David Gall, a research medical officer, found the cause of death. When he first examined the grisly sample, he saw what he took to be the head of a pin. He thought that it had been placed to mark a point from which a pathologist could orientate his examination, but when he touched it with his finger, it rolled down into the fluid channel of the pathology table. Before it could disappear down the drain he picked it up and placed it in a specimen jar for examination later. When looked at closely, it proved to be a tiny bead of metal with two holes drilled into it at right angles to each other.

This mysterious item was now sent to the Metropolitan Police Forensic Science Laboratory at Lambeth, where it was examined in detail by Dr Robin Keeley, the scientist in charge of the Scanning Electron Microscope Unit. When it appeared on the television monitor, it could clearly be seen what an ingenious method of killing had been used.

It was a tiny alloy pellet which had carried the poison that killed Markov. It was only 1.53 mm in diameter, smaller than the head of a pin. The two holes in it measured 0.33 mm, and it was calculated that it would have contained approximately 0.5 mg of some type of poisonous substance. The alloy was an amalgam of platinum and iridium, which the body would not naturally reject. But this was only the vehicle which had carried the killing agent. What was the poison that had been used, and how had it been injected into the body? The search began to find the answers to these questions.

As no traces of a toxic agent had been found in the body tissues, it was necessary to first discover from what group the poison came that had been used to kill Markov. Had an inorganic poison such as cyanide or arsenic been used? It was not possible. More such poison would be necessary to kill a person of Markov's stature than the pellet could contain.

Could it have been an organic poison such as nicotine or fluoro-acetate? Again it would need at least 10 mg to kill a man, and the pellet was just not large enough to contain that amount of poison.

A nerve gas? The amount needed to kill a man was very close to the capacity of the tiny ball. No. These agents produce a characteristic disruption of the nervous system, and none of these signs could be detected in Markov's case.

Was there a chance that a bio-toxin had been responsible? This was highly likely. Bio-toxins are a group of poisonous substances that occur naturally in plants and animals. Their effect on the body would be very similar to what had been observed during the victim's protracted death. The bio-toxins include substances that cause diphtheria, tetanus and botulism. It can be found in the rosemary pea that grows in Africa, and it can also be found in snake venom.

There is one particular poison that was considered at quite

an early stage in the inquiry as being the likely culprit. This is the poison known as ricin, which is derived from the husk of the castor-oil bean. A series of tests were carried out and the conclusion was that this was the most likely agent to have been used. Yet it was not possible to say positively that it *was* the cause, as no trace of the poison was ever found in the body or in the pellet.

That left one more mystery to be cleared up. How had the pellet containing the poison been injected into Markov's leg? After he had been struck, he had turned round and seen a man picking up an umbrella. Had the means of firing and injecting the pellet been concealed in this everyday accessory? The answer is that it *was* possible – a gas or an air gun could have been hidden in the shaft.

In the absence of a definite identification of the poison, and the inability to produce the weapon, it would be very difficult to prove in a court of law exactly how Georgi Markov died. But there has been a breakthrough. Since the political and social changes that have taken place in Europe, the authorities in Bulgaria have admitted responsibility for causing Markov's death. They have promised that there will be a full inquiry into what happened, and it is said that those responsible will stand trial. It has taken many years for the truth to emerge.

For some time the pellet was housed in a sealed phial in one of the cabinets in the Black Museum. It was the smallest item there and yet one which was of abiding interest – in a way a small token to posterity of a country's injustice to one man, who only preached the freedom that we take for granted. Now, in view of the potential inquiry into the incident, the pellet has been temporarily removed from the museum as it constitutes valuable evidence. It is just possible that someone may at some time in the future stand trial for the murder of a man who stood up for his principles.

17

THE CHRONOLOGY OF SERIAL KILLER DENNIS NILSEN

Every day we are disgusted when we hear of violent multiple deaths. It poses the question in our minds as to why do people kill their fellow human beings and why do some continue to kill again and again? What causes someone to suddenly strike against the norms of the society we live in? They are questions which psychiatrists, criminologists, police officers and psychologists would dearly like to answer. They would like to have them resolved with sufficient precision to enable them to identify the latent potential of the killer in society.

There are a number of defined motives for murder. Jealousy which creates distorted images and ideas in the mind of a person, whereby the only outlet they can conceive of is to kill the object of their tangled thoughts. The threat upon one person by another is perceived to be overwhelming and the only solution appears to be to eliminate that threat. Then there are greed and avarice, where the temptation of personal gain and the need to prevent anything standing in the way of achieving that goal must be erased. Also, the motive of revenge, where retaliation for an offence or injury caused by one individual to another, results in the idea of getting one's own back on whoever is conceived as being responsible.

Sexual gratification is another motive. Regardless of any other point of view, they believe that their convictions are the right ones and anyone opposing them should be killed. The large majority of murders are committed by people known or related to the victim and are often committed in fits of pique or drunkenness. These are not difficult to solve. It is the murders where the killer has no association with his victim, selecting them at random from the population at large that prove to be the most difficult to resolve.

Are serial killers the result of their background and upbringing, where the experiences of their lives have so traumatically scarred their personalities and numbed their sensitivities, that murder becomes the way of getting their own back on society? Or is it the need to gratify their egos? After all what is the point of being the most prolific serial killer in the world if the world does not know. Could it be a social phenomena brought about by the pressures and complexity of the world we live in?

Here is a chronography of Dennis Nilsen. It is an interesting insight into the progress of his life and what may have motivated him to kill again and again, and yet again.

1942–1961

2 May 42	Betty Whyte (mother) married Olav Magnus Nilsen (father). Lived at 47, Academy Road, Fraserburgh, with parents Andrew and Lily Whyte.
12 Mar 43	Brother Olav born.
23 Nov 45	Dennis born.
29 Aug 48	Sister Sylvia born.
1948	Parents divorced.
1950	Started school at Fraserburgh Infants.
31 Oct 51	Grandfather, aged 62, died of a heart attack at sea.
1951–52	Family moved to council flat at 73, Mid Street, Fraserburgh.

4 Nov 54	Mother married Adam Scott, a labourer.
8 Apr 55	Half-sister Violet born.
1955	Family moved to 16, Baird Road, Strichen, Aberdeenshire. Enrolled at Strichen Secondary School, with his brother and sister.
1956	Half-brother Andrew born.
10 Nov 57	Half-brother Gordon born.
1958	Joined Strichen Army Cadet Corps.
16 Nov 1959	Half-brother Morris born.
1961	Left school. Obtained work with Maconachie's Fish Cannery, Fraserburgh.
28 Jun 61	Enlisted in the Army in Aberdeen. Signed on for 9 years
6 Sep 61	Joined the Army as an apprentice chef. Army No. 23874391, Army Catering Corps 'A' Company, Junior Leaders Regiment.

Events in Nilsen's formative years were responsible for the personality that he developed in his adult life. He never remembered his father, and his mother spent little time giving him the love and affection so important in childhood. His grandfather provided the role model for him, spending a lot of time making kites for the boy and taking him for long walks. Andrew Whyte spoilt his grandson and Nilsen had fond childhood memories of him. Nilsen was three when he was found wandering the streets looking for his grandfather, not understanding that Whyte was away at sea. When Whyte died, the boy was allowed to see his grandfather's body. It is certain that seeing the corpse of the man for whom he had the greatest affection had a very deep effect on the six-year-old. As with most young children, he was not told that his grandfather was dead and assumed he was just asleep. The gradual realisation that his grandfather would not be coming home again emotionally destroyed him and he grew into a retiring and introverted child, happier with his own company than with that of others. To compound the situation, his mother's re-marriage produced feelings of resentment in Nilsen, although he later grew to respect his stepfather.

When he was ten, he and some other boys formed an interest in pigeons which they raised in a disused air-raid shelter. Going to feed the birds one day, he found that someone had killed them. This incident was to have a long-lasting effect. The boy had an interest in and an affinity for animals which he was never allowed to develop, except for a rabbit, which he kept in a small hutch. When it died he was accused of starving it to death.

Ironically it was animals that gave him his first experiences of killing. He would spend long hours walking in the countryside surrounding his home, and when the epidemic of myxomatosis was at its worst, any rabbit that he found suffering with the disease he would dispatch, rather than see it subjected to further pain. He felt acutely the poverty of his family circumstances, but within the limits of their finances his parents gave him as good an upbringing as possible.

1961–63	These years were spent training in soldiery and his chosen trade as a cook.

1964

25 May	Passing-out parade. Sent on leave. Had an accident on a hired scooter. Taken to infirmary with superficial head injuries and bruises, and later discharged.
25 Sept	Posted to 1st Battalion, Royal Fusiliers, at BAOR, Osnabrück, in Germany, as a Catering Corps cook.
Sept–Dec 64	Beaten up in a fight with a corporal, after lunch-time drinking session.

1965

27 May	Returned to UK to attend cook's upgrading course.
23 July	Completed course. Promoted to lance-corporal.
18 Aug	Returned to Germany.
12 Nov	Attended junior NCOs' course.

1966

Early 1966	Went to Norway with regiment.
22 July	Promoted to corporal.
24 Dec	Unit returned to the UK. Taken on the strength of Depot Training Battalion, Aldershot, as a cook.

1967

18 Jan	Posted to Aden to Military Provost Staff Corps, 518 company, at Al Mansoura Detention Centre, as a cook.
21 July	Posted in charge of catering to the Trucial Oman Scouts' Mess, at Sharjah in the Persian Gulf.

1968

15 Jan	Returned to UK, and posted to 1st Battalion, the Argyll and Sutherland Highlanders, Seaton Barracks, Plymouth.
17 Sept	Sent to Cyprus with unit on Exercise 'Shipowner'.

1969

15 April   Unit posted to Berlin, where he was in
                  charge of catering for the officers' mess at
                  Montgomery Barracks.

1970

Jan–Feb   Sent to Bodenmais in Bavaria, to cater for
                  ski-training parties.
28 May   Unit returned to Fort George, Scotland.
1 June   Attended management course No 3 at
                  Aldershot.
Aug–Sept   Posted to Royal Guard, Ballater, as Catering
                  NCO.

1971

24 Jan   Posted to 242 Squadron, Royal Corps of
                  Signals, Aces High Station, Massey Hill,
                  Shetland Isles, as a cook.
13 Oct   Attended a two-day projectionist course at
                  Beaconsfield.

1972

30 April   Charged with entertaining civilians on army
                  premises at 1.40am for which he was
                  reprimanded.
Summer   Formed an affection for another soldier.
22 Nov   Discharged from the army at his own
                  request, and placed on the reserve. He left as
                  a substantive Corporal, having been awarded
                  the General Service Medal for the time spent

in South Arabia. He went to live at 16, Baird
Road, Strichen, with his family.

18 Dec   Joined the Metropolitan Police and went to
Hendon Training School for his initial
training. Warrant Number 164305.

1973

9 April   Posted to Willesden Police Station.
Divisional Number 287. Lived in the section
house. During the month he was taken into a
mortuary as part of his training by his parent
constable.

5 July   Applied to join the 'Campaign for
Homosexual Equality'.

20 Aug   Olav Magnus Moksheim, alias Nilsen, his
father, died in Ghana.

6 Dec   Employed by the Department of
Employment, as a property security guard.

9 Dec   Officially resigned from the Metropolitan
Police.

These years of Nilsen's life were probably the ones he most
identified with. He achieved in his army career a sense of purpose which he had never experienced before. He found that
the comradeship in the service gave him the opportunity of
making friends which he had missed in his younger years. He
also found that the responsibilities of his life as an army cook
suited him. It was the time when he formed his adult personality. From being introspective and a loner, he now found
he could express himself in his work, and that he enjoyed the
company of the men around him. It was also the time when
he first realised that his affections towards men were stronger
than his feelings towards women.

Nilsen was greatly disappointed after leaving the army to
join the police. He found the comradeship completely different

to that which he had experienced in the services. While tightly
knit during working hours, it did not extend to life when off
duty. Life in the police section house was not the same as in
army barracks. Outside interests were essential, and in the
search for these Nilsen entered the twilight world of homo-
sexuality.

He visited bars, meeting men who had the same problems
with relationships as himself. London, for all the pleasures
that it has to offer, and the high density of population that it
contains, can be a very lonely place when you have no friends
and find difficulty in communicating. Many people who live
in large cities find the same coldness in their lives when they
leave their working environment and return to their homes. It
was during this period that Nilsen set the mould for what was
to be the pattern of his life. He rebelled against himself, inter-
nalised his feelings, and withdrew within himself, finding
very little pleasure from the activities that he engaged in.
Joining the police was an unconscious attempt to normalise
and discipline himself against the urges that were building up
within him. The sense of rejection that he experienced was
going to prove too much for him.

1974

16 Jan	He was informed of his father's death, and learned that he had inherited a little over £1000.
13 Feb	Moved to 80, Teignmouth Road, NW2.
8 May	Resigned from his security job, because of the unsocial hours.
20 May	Obtained a job with the Civil Service as a clerical assistant with the Manpower Services Commission, working at the Job Centre, 1–3 Denmark Street, WC 2.
11 May	Attended a training course at Hanway House.

November	Seen walking down the road arm in arm with another man.

1975

January	Became CPSA Union rep at Denmark Street.
3 March	Was assaulted in the Job Centre by a Mr John Hall. Took out a private summons, and Hall was sentenced to 7 months' detention.
19 Aug	Took a 17-year-old boy David Painter back to his flat and made sexual advances to him. The boy lost his temper, and Nilsen called the police. Went to Willesden Green Police Station where he was questioned about the cause of the incident, and as there was no evidence of interference, he was released, and no charges were made against him.
November	Met David Gallichan and took him home. They agreed to form a relationship.
22 Nov	Moved to 195, Melrose Avenue, NW2.

1976

10 Feb	Sick with abdominal pains.
23 Feb	Referred to Willesden Hospital. Suffered acute abdominal pain until June.
Spring	Gallichan purchased a dog which Nilsen named 'Bleep'
16 June	Operated on for gallstones at Willesden General Hospital.
Xmas	Took Gallichan to a Xmas party at Denmark Street.

1977

May	Gallichan moved out of the flat at Melrose Avenue.
Summer	Met Barry Pett in William IV public house, who a few weeks later moved in with him.
November	Nilsen met Steven Martin at the Golden Lion public house, took him home. This was to be a close relationship. Martin would visit Nilsen at work, and together they frequented a gay club. Xmas was spent together at home.

These four years were a period of some considerable trauma for Nilsen. His attempts to form a permanent domestic relationship with Gallichan were a bitter-sweet experience for him. Nilsen paid most of the bills during the time they were together, and their relationship soured when Gallichan began to bring strangers back to the flat. The association ended in acrimony and remorse.

Although Nilsen had a permanent job in the Civil Service, and had been appointed union representative, he found the latter position was not what he had hoped for. He experienced rejection at all levels – by those senior to him because of what he represented, and by those who had elected him, who showed little interest in what he was doing for them. His nagging stomach illness and periods of sickness left him feeling low and depressed. He formed a number of casual associations during these years, but they gave him little satisfaction.

The new year of 1978 was when his real problems began to manifest themselves. Disillusioned, he turned to the ultimate crime, strangely as a source of relief, an outlet for his frustrations.

1978

January	Nilsen returned to his flat with an 18-year-old youth, who left during the night stealing some money and property.
9 Feb	Martin moved out.
11 Feb	Nilsen met Martin again at Cine Arts Club, and the latter returned home with him.
14 Feb	Went again to the Cine Arts Club, where he had a big row with Martin and told him to move out.
16 Feb	Martin collected his belongings and again moved out. Met a Swiss au pair girl, and took her back to the flat.
11 Apr	Had a disagreement at the Job Centre.
18 May	Two associates from work visited him at his flat.
20 May	Considered for promotion but turned down as unsuitable, because of problems relating to his personality and attitude.
May–June	Period of sickness.
August	Martin returned to Melrose Avenue, to collect a parcel.
9–15 Sept	Attended CPSA Chairman's School, at Surrey University, and enjoyed mixing with senior union officials. Came home to find that a man from Liverpool who he had entrusted with the keys of his flat, had stolen his camera and projector and broken into the gas and electricity meters.
13 Oct	As a result of the Gay Switchboard Flatshare Linkup, Paul Dermody stayed with Nilsen at the flat for a fortnight.
Nov–Dec	Periods of sick leave.
20 Dec	Office Xmas party at Denmark Street. Nilsen cooked a curry meal for Job Centre staff. Supplied a pot, and an electric carving knife.

29 Dec	VICTIM 1. Met unidentified Irishman 17–18 years old at the Cricklewood Arms public house. Took him home. Strangled him, and concealed body under the floorboards.

1979

4 Jan	Injured shoulder and was X-rayed at hospital. Followed by a period of sickness. Employed in the self-service Job Centre.
April	Attended a weekend Union course at Egham. Followed by a period of sickness.
May	Attended CPSA Conference at Southport.
12 July	Acting Executive Officer, in charge of section at the Job Centre.
28 July	Working in marketing section of Job Centre.
30 July	Appointed Acting Executive Officer.
11 Aug	Burnt the body of first victim, on waste ground at back of flat.
3 Sept	Phoned Information Room to report a robbery.
13 Oct	Took Andrew Ho back to the flat, where he wanted to indulge in bondage. Put a cord round Ho's neck and tightened it. Ho broke free and informed the police, but would not prefer charges.
November	Went to special conference at Southport.
3 Dec	VICTIM 2. Met Kenneth James Ockenden, aged 23, a Canadian, in the Princess Louise public house. Took him home and strangled him with flex of stereo headphones. Put body under floorboards three days later.
4 Dec	Reported sick.

By now Nilsen had embarked on a road from which there was no turning back. The world of the serial killer is a conflict between normality and insanity. It manifests itself with bouts of depression and swings of mood. It is a disturbance of the function of the brain and central nervous system, rather than actual damage to the brain tissue, giving rise to functional psychoses, which lead to a wide variety of mental illnesses, resulting in varied and irrational behaviour. The problem of dealing with this type of killer is in determining whether the acts of killing are committed with controlled intent, or whether they are motivated by one of the periods of disassociation from reality, which personalities of this type are subject to. It is very difficult in cases of serious crime which remain undetected for some time to determine in retrospect exactly what the perpetrator's mental condition was. It becomes difficult for the defence in such cases to introduce evidence of insanity, when in court the defendant appears to be perfectly normal.

To those who are not informed about the intricacies of this type of defence, such attempts at proving insanity at the time of the offence are often dismissed as psychological mumbo jumbo. In fact it is an endeavour to prove the existence of a very identifiable mental condition known as diminished responsibility, which means that the offender was normal both before and after the crime but at the time it was committed he/she was not. In cases like Nilsen's where someone kills a number of people one after the other, there has to be some degree of mental abnormality when compared with the normal behaviour of the man in the street, and attempting to prove otherwise must be treated with a certain amount of scepticism.

1980

Early 1980   Had associations with a number of men.
                   Seen in hotel threatening another man.

Mar/Apr	Periods of sickness.
30 April	Arrested for drunkenness.
1 May	Case dismissed at court.
9 May	Attended Union conference at Southport. Left his dog in care of a friend.
16 May	Collected dog.
17 May	VICTIM 3. Picked up Martyn Duffey, 16, took him home and strangled him with a tie. When he found Duffey was still alive, carried him into kitchen, and held his head under water until dead. Put body in a cupboard, and then under the floorboards.
Summer	Seen with facial scratches and a black eye. Could possibly be associated with victim 3.
August	VICTIM 4. Picked up a William David Sutherland, 25, in the West End; took him to Melrose Avenue where he strangled him.
26 Aug	Present at a Union picket at Brixton.
28 Aug	Reported sick with exhaustion.
3 Sept	Reported sick again.
October	VICTIM 5. Met a man described by Nilsen as either a Mexican or Filipino in the Cricklewood Arms public house. Taken to Melrose Avenue and strangled.
9 Oct	Attended Union conference, at Great Russell Street.
10 Oct	Reported sick.
Autumn	VICTIM 6. Met an Irishman (unknown) in the Cricklewood Arms public house, took him home and strangled him. Placed the body under the floorboards that night. VICTIM 7. Met a vagrant in Charing Cross Road, at the junction with Oxford Street, late in the evening. Took him back in a taxi to Melrose Avenue where he was strangled, dismembered and placed under the floorboards.
Late Autumn	Removed the bodies of victims 2, 3, 4, 5, 6,

7, from under the floorboards, carried them wrapped in a piece of old carpet to some waste ground at the back of the flat, where over a period of days he burnt them in a series of bonfires. He burnt old car tyres with the bodies to disguise the smell. Local children stood and watched while he tended the fire. At some time during this period he reported sick, and then took some leave and worked as a cook at a diner in Endell Street.

10 Nov   Met Douglas Stewart and another man in the Golden Lion public house. Took Stewart back to his flat, and tried to murder him. Stewart left flat at 4am, and reported incident to the police, who visited the flat but dealt with it as a homosexual encounter.

11 Nov   Sick for seven days. This possibly related to one of the killings.

Nov–Dec   VICTIM 8. Met him in the West End, after the pubs had shut. Took him home to Melrose Avenue, strangled him, and placed the body under the floor. Later he dissected the body.

Xmas   Cooked a curry meal for the staff at the Job Centre. Provided a cooking pot and an electric carving knife. Cleaned up the following day.

It is interesting to note that while Nilsen was vague when asked to describe the exact dates when he murdered his victims, he invariably reported sick or took leave after he had killed someone, or when he was disposing of the bodies.

1981

Early Jan   VICTIM 9. Met him at the Golden Lion public house, took him to Melrose Avenue by

	taxi, killed him by strangulation with a tie, and placed him under the floorboards.
12 Jan	Reported sick. Removed the body of victim 9 from beneath the floor and dissected it, using ordinary kitchen knives.
February	VICTIM 10. Met him in West End. Again, strangled him with a tie, and placed the body under the floorboards.
13 Mar	Attended a Union meeting in West Ham.
Easter	Arranged film show at Denmark Street.
April	VICTIM 11. Met skinhead in Leicester Square, and took him for a meal. Then took him by taxi to Melrose Avenue, where he strangled him, and placed the body under the floorboards.
Early May	He became worried about the smell. Lifted the bodies from under the floorboards, dissected them and disposed of the results on the waste ground at the back of the house, and some in the rubbish bin.
May	Attended a Union conference at Brighton.
30 May	Alleged theft from his flat while at conference.
26 June	Returned from conference to find that his flat had been robbed, and damaged with creosote. Granted £200 from a staff welfare fund, to assist in repairing the damage.
4 July	Went to a CPSA Union meeting at Denmark House.
7 July	Attended an Aliens course at Bryan House.
27 July	Given a cheque, the proceeds of a staff collection, to pay for the damage to his flat.
28 July	Applied for promotion to EO.
4 Aug	Sick.
August	Removed the bodies of victims 8, 9, 10, 11 from under the floorboards, dissected the bodies of his last three victims (he had

	already dealt with victim 8). Wrapped the pieces up in separate bundles, and replaced them under the floor. The internal organs he dumped on waste ground.
18 Sept	VICTIM 12. Malcolm Barlow aged 26, found outside the house in Melrose Avenue apparently ill. Nilsen called an ambulance and he was taken to hospital.
19 Sept	Barlow was discharged from hospital and returned to Melrose Avenue. Nilsen took him in, strangled him and put him under the floorboards.
4 Oct	Removed victims 8, 9, 10, 11, and 12 from under the floorboards, took them to the waste land at the back of the house, and burnt them.
5 Oct	Moved to 23, Cranley Gardens, N10, having been paid £1000 to leave Melrose Avenue so that the house could be renovated.
9 Oct	Found a man drunk in the West End. Took him home for the night, nothing happened.
15 Oct	Attended Union meeting.
23 Nov	Met Paul Nobbs in Golden Lion public house. Visited Foyles bookshop, and then went to Cranley Gardens. During the night he attempted to strangle him.
December	Met 'John the Guardsman' in a pub in the West End. Although nothing occurred on this occasion, he would later become a victim. During the month he met a number of men, some of whom stayed with him at Cranley Gardens. Nothing occurred.

Another year where Nilsen continued with his killings. There were also a number of occasions where people visited the house, stayed the night, and left in the morning. Nilsen later

said that what gave him the urge to kill was drinking Bacardi
and coke. There is little to suggest that this was other than an
excuse.

1982

12 Jan	Went to a Union meeting at Bryan House.
21 Jan	Went to a Union meeting again at Bryan House.
28 Jan	Went to a Union meeting at Manway House.
2 Feb	Nilsen was robbed by three men in Muswell Hill Road.
February	During the month he lost his post as the Union rep to Miss Hughes.
March	Came home late and knocked up other residents, because he had lost his key. Drunken youth ejected by police from 23, Cranley Gardens at 3am. Gave an electric carving knife to a girl at work. VICTIM 13. Met 'John the Guardsman', John Peter Howlett aged 23, again in the Salisbury public house, took him to 23, Cranley Gardens where he murdered him. First he tried to strangle him, but only succeeded in rendering him unconscious. He managed to carry Howlett to the bathroom, where he filled the bath, and held his head under the water.
9 April	A man called Knox visits and stays for eight days. They tour London and visit the Salisbury and Golden Lion public houses.
May	Met Carl Stotter in the Black Cap public house in Camden High Street, took him back to 23, Cranley Gardens where he attempted to strangle him. Stotter woke up with the dog

	Bleep licking his face, and a red mark around his neck.
June	Miss Bridges moves into first-floor flat of 23, Cranley Gardens.
28 June	Promoted to EO, and transferred to the Job Centre at Kentish Town.
30 June	Went to a staff drinks party at Abbey Tavern, Kentish Town. Stayed the night in a flat at Park Hill Road. Slept on the floor.
July	Man stayed with Nilsen for four days.
Sept	VICTIM 14. Met Archibald Graham Allen in Shaftesbury Avenue, Wl. Took him to 23, Cranley Gardens where he was murdered.
9 Oct	Sick. Was seen with various men.
3 Dec	Tried to pick up man in Muswell Hill Road.
22 Dec	Picked up Trevor Simpson who stayed with him over Xmas.
27 Dec	Simpson woke up to find the room was filled with smoke. Found a pair of jeans on fire in the room which Nilsen told him he had set on fire when he went to sleep while smoking a cigarette.
31 Dec	Nilsen invited the two girls from downstairs to his flat for New Year drink. They declined. Met Toshimitso Ozawa in the Green Man public house, took him to 23, Cranley Gardens where he attempted to strangle him. Ozawa ran out of the house.

1983

3 Jan	Seen in the King William public house at Hampstead.
22–26 Jan	Believed to have picked up Sinclair in Shaftesbury Avenue.
1 Feb	VICTIM 15. Met Stephen Neil Sinclair in

the Royal George public house, in Goslett
Yard. Took him home to 23, Cranley
Gardens and strangled him with a tie,
reinforced with string. Cut up the body on a
plastic sheet in the front room. Put the head
in a cooking pot and boiled it on the stove in
the kitchen.

3 Feb	Other residents find toilets blocked. Noises heard in Nilsen's flat.
4 Feb	Nilsen complains to estate agents about the blocked drains.
5 Feb	Friend visits 23, Cranley Gardens and Nilsen refuses to let him in.
6 Feb	Plumber tries to clear the drains and fails.
8 Feb	Nilsen writes a letter to the estate agents, complaining about the drains. Dyno-Rod find flesh in the drain.
9 Feb	Nilsen heard outside removing drain cover. Seen wearing Sinclair's scarf, at Job Centre, Kentish Town. Miss Bridges contacts the police. Nilsen arrested by Detective Chief Inspector Jay at 5.40pm, when he arrived home from work.
11 Feb	Nilsen charged with the murder of Stephen Neil Sinclair. Remanded in Brixton Prison. Number B62006.
March	Dog Bleep died in dogs' home. Pined away.
21 Apr	Appeared at Highgate Magistrates' Court and said that he wished to discharge legal aid; told his solicitor, Mr Ronald Moss, that he would defend himself.
28 Apr	Appeared at Highgate for committal proceedings without legal representation.
9 May	Nilsen wrote a letter formally resigning from the Civil Service.
22 May	Date from which resignation took effect.
July	Refused to wear his prison uniform.

1 Aug	In a fit of temper threw the contents of his chamber pot over prison officers, and in the scuffle that ensued, he got a black eye and lost a tooth.
5 Aug	Appeared at the Old Bailey; announced his intention of re-instructing his solicitor, Mr Ronald Moss.
9 Aug	Adjudication panel heard charges of offences against prison discipline. Given 56 days' punishment, and loss of privileges, for assaulting prison officers.
19 Sept	Dismissed his solicitor, who was replaced by Mr Ralph Haeems.
24 Oct	Trial opened in number one court at the Old Bailey.
4 Nov	At 4.23pm, the jury returned a verdict of guilty by a majority of 10–2, on 6 charges of murder and 2 of attempted murder. Jury out for 12 hours 26 minutes. Sentenced to life imprisonment, with a recommendation that he should not be released for 25 years. Sent to Wormwood Scrubs.

Dennis Nilsen spends his life in comparative isolation. While in remand prison he wrote over two hundred letters, mostly making points about his rights as a prisoner or drawing attention to his treatment.

While in the Scrubs he was slashed across the face by another prisoner, the wound requiring a number of stitches. It was said that he did not respond when it happened, just stood still looking straight ahead. He has since been moved to other prisons, where he has to be kept on a special wing for fear of attack by other prisoners, who would gain kudos in the prison hierachy for such an assault.

Nilsen would not say exactly how many men he killed, but he thought fifteen or sixteen. There is a possibility that there were as many as eighteen victims.

In theory Nilsen should *never* be released from prison, having been sentenced to life imprisonment, but this does not always cover an individual's natural life span. If he served just the minimum period of twenty-five years recommended by the judge, it means he would be sixty-three when released.

Case Facts

NAME:	Dennis Nilsen.
DATE OF BIRTH:	23 November 1945
VICTIMS (known):	Kenneth Ockenden *He was charged with the*
	Martyn Duffey *murder of these six. There*
	Billy Sutherland *were others who were not*
	Malcolm Barlow *identified, and others he*
	John Howlett *admitted killing, but which*
	Stephen Sinclair *could not be proved.*
DETECTIVES:	Detective Chief Superintendent Geoffrey Chambers
	Detective Superintendent Norman Briers
	Detective Chief Inspector Peter Jay
	Detective Sergeant Steve McCusker
CROWN COUNSEL:	Mr Allan Green
	Mr Julian Bevan
DEFENCE COUNSEL:	Mr Ivan Lawrence QC, MP
	Mr Robert Flach
JUDGE:	Mr Justice Croom-Johnson
SENTENCE:	Life imprisonment, with a recommendation that he serves at least 25 years.

APPENDIX I

COMMISSIONERS OF THE METROPOLITAN POLICE

The Commissioner is appointed by the Sovereign, acting on the advice of the Home Secretary of the day. As the Chief Officer of the Police, he is in overall command of the Metropolitan Police, and responsible for all police operations in London. As such he is independent of governmental control, and answerable to the law for all his actions.

7 July 1829	Colonel Sir Charles Rowan KCB and Sir Richard Mayne KCB, appointed as joint Commissioners.
5 Jan 1850	Rowan retired.
6 Jan 1850	Capt. William Hay appointed joint Commissioner with Mayne.
29 Aug 1855	Capt. Hay died.
26 Dec 1868	Sir Richard Mayne died, in office.
27 Dec 1868	Colonel D.W.P Labolmondiere, CB, appointed Acting Commissioner.
13 Feb 1869	Colonel Edmund Henderson, KCB, RE, appointed Commissioner .
26 Mar 1886	Henderson resigned.

29 Mar 1886	General Sir Charles Warren, GCMG, KCB, RE, FRS, appointed as Commissioner.
1 Dec 1888	Warren resigned.
3 Dec 1888	James Monro CB returned to the force having resigned in August 1888, and appointed Commissioner.
21 Jun 1890	Monro resigned. He had been in office 19 months.
23 Jun 1890	Colonel Sir Edward Bradford, Bt, GCB, GCVO, KCSI appointed Commissioner.
4 Mar 1903	Bradford retired.
31 May 1903	Sir Edward Henry, Bt, GCVO, KCB, CSI appointed Commissioner.
31 Aug 1918	Henry resigned, after being made scapegoat for police strike.
31 Aug 1918	General Sir Nevil Macready, Bt, GCMG, KCB appointed Commissioner. Announced in the evening of the same day that Henry resigned.
April 1920	Macready resigned. He had been in office 20 months.
April 1920	Brigadier General Sir William Horwood GBE, KCB, DSO appointed Commissioner.
7 Nov 1928	Horwood retired.
8 Nov 1928	General (later Field Marshal) the Rt Hon Lord Byng of Vimy, GCB, GCMG, MVO, LL D appointed Commissioner.
30 Sept 1931	Lord Byng retired on account of ill health.
2 Nov 1931	Marshal of the Royal Air Force the Lord Trenchard, GCB, DSO, DCL, LL D appointed Commissioner.
11 Nov 1935	Lord Trenchard retired.
29 Nov 1935	Air Vice-Marshal Sir Philip W. Game, GCB, GCVO appointed Commissioner.
31 May 1945	Sir Philip Game retired.

1 June 1945	Sir Harold Scott, KCB, KBE, a Civil Servant, appointed Commissioner.
13 Aug 1953	Sir Harold Scott retired.
14 Aug 1953	Sir John R.H. Nott Bower, KCVO appointed Commissioner.
31 Aug 1958	Sir John Nott Bower retired.
1 Sept 1958	Sir Joseph Simpson, KBE appointed Commissioner.
20 Mar 1968	Sir Joseph Simpson died, in office.
21 Mar 1968	Sir John Waldron, KCVO, the Deputy Commissioner, appointed Commissioner.
16 April 1972	Sir John Waldron retired.
17 April 1972	Sir Robert Mark, GBE, QPM appointed Commissioner.
12 Mar 1977	Sir Robert Mark retired.
13 Mar 1977	Sir David McNee, QPM appointed Commissioner.
1 Oct 1982	Sir David McNee retired.
2 Oct 1982	Sir Kenneth Newman, QPM, LLB, FBIM appointed Commissioner.
1 Aug 1987	Sir Kenneth Newman retired.
2 Aug 1987	Sir Peter Imbert, QPM appointed Commissioner.
1 Feb 1993	Sir Peter Imbert retired.
1 Feb 1993	Paul Condon QPM appointed Commissioner.

APPENDIX 2

DESCRIPTIVE WORDS FOR THE POLICE

The Bill | This has a number of possible derivations. It may have referred to the tipstaff which was carried by the police to denote their office. Inside was contained their warrant to arrest, which was often referred to as a 'Bill'. If you were touched with the tipstaff it signified that you were being taken into custody.

The Bill is also the term given by cabdrivers to the licence issued by the Metropolitan Police authorising them to apply for hire.

After the First World War, Old Bill, a cartoon character, was used in advertisements for police recruits.

Today, *The Bill* is the title of a television series, and in consequence has come into popular use.

Bluebottles | Colloquial English, used to refer to Beadles or Constables. References can be found in Shakespeare as far back as 1597. Used a lot in the 1800s and the early part of the twentieth century.

Blue Devils — First seen on a broadsheet. Descriptive of the uniform.

Bobbies — Reference to Sir Robert Peel.

Bogies — In common use pre-1914.

Brain — Detective. Used by other police officers.

Busy/Busies — Cant for detective or CID officer. Used since the early l900s.

Chut Chai — Chinese triad slang for policeman. Translated literally means 'pawn'.

Cops — Because they 'copped' people.

Coppers — Again the reason is because they 'copped' or arrested people. Has become one of the most used terms for describing policemen.

Copmen — Term used in Australia. Derived as above.

Cozzer — Used by barrow boys since 1930s. Derives from the Hebrew 'chazer', a pig.

Crushers — A reference to the heavy-footed interference with the liberty of the subject.

Dick — American term

Esclop — Nineteenth-century term. Probably back slang. Sometimes the E and C are omitted, and the word 'slop' is used.

Escop — As above in slightly shortened form.

Fla Yiu — Triad slang for policeman. Literal meaning is 'flowery waist'.

Flatfoot — Referring to a policeman's pedal extremities. In common use in 1935.

Flatties — From the above.

Flic	From the French.
The Filth	Slang expression which has been in use since the 1950s. Often used by confirmed criminals.
Fuzz	Canadian term, first heard late 1950s, but used in this country by early 1960s. Probably derives from the similarity with the parasitic mould found on rotting food, rather than the whiskers once commonly worn by policemen.
Gendarme	From the French.
Grunter	Slang for policeman.
Hundred to-oner	This reference comes from a horse called 'Bastard' that came in at a hundred to one. Nineteenth-century.
Jackdaw	Rhyming slang for the law.
Jack	Shortened form of above.
Jocks	Eighteenth-century term for a detective.
Jockeys	As above.
Judy Scuffer	Policewoman. Mainly used in Liverpool.
The Law	Self-explanatory.
Miltonian	Reference to the polish on boots. Milton was the brand name of a shoe polish.
Nick Nick	Used by Jim Davidson, the comedian, when performing one of his comic routines. Became a catch phrase, and was accompanied by a movement of holding the hand to the forehead, and opening and closing the fingers. In common usage in the 1970s and 1980s.
Peelers	Reference to Sir Robert Peel.
Peel's Bloody Gang	An early reference, used by those who

	were upset at the formation of the police.
Pigs	Cant for a policeman or detective used as far back as 1820s. Revived early 1960s by the counter culture. As a term it is intended to incite; it seldom does. Often interpreted by police as being the abbreviation for Perfectly Integrated Gentleman.
Raw Lobsters	Used when police first appeared on the on the streets of London. It referred to their blue swallow-tailed coats.
Robert	Reference to Sir Robert Peel.
Robin Redbreasts	A reference to the mounted police force formed in 1805, because they wore scarlet waistcoats as part of their uniform.
Rozzers	Believed to come from the north of England.
Rossers	As above.
Scuffer	Liverpool term for policeman.
Scufter	North country expression.
Uncle Bill	Term in use in the 1930s.
Uncle Bob	From Bobbies.

SELECT BIBLIOGRAPHY

Scotland Yard: its History and Organisation 1829–1929, George Dilnot. Published by Geoffrey Bles. Editions 1926, 1927, 1929.

The Queen's Peace, David Ascoli. Hamish Hamilton 1979.

The Rise of Scotland Yard, Douglas G. Browne. George G. Harrap 1956.

The First Detectives, Belton Cobb. Faber and Faber 1957.

Policing The Victorian Community, by Carolyn Steedman. Routledge and Kegan Paul 1984.

The Fingerprint Story, by Gerald Lambourne. Harrap 1984.

Murder Under the Microscope, Philip Paul. Macdonald 1990.

Notable British Trials Series, edited by Harry Hodge. William Hodge.

INDEX